THE AUSTRALIANS

THE AUSTRALIANS

RODNEY HALL

Photograph selection and captions:
René Gordon

First published 1984 by
Lloyd O'Neil Pty Ltd
56 Claremont Street
South Yarra
Victoria, Australia
for Currey O'Neil

Designers René Gordon, Zoë Gent-Murphy
Typeset by Tricia Randle

ISBN 0 85550 810 8

Printed in Hong Kong

Distributed by Gordon and Gotch Ltd
Melbourne, Sydney, Adelaide, Brisbane,
Perth, Launceston

Author's Acknowledgements

Firstly I would like to thank Tony Barratt who has been a marvellously patient researcher, suffering late night calls and remaining unshakable even when presented with obscure queries. I am also grateful to John Thompson of the National Library of Australia, Bill Fewer of the Woden Library, the staff of the Australian Institute of Aboriginal Studies, the Australian War Memorial, and to Rosalie Hannink.

Rodney Hall
Bermagui South, 1984

Publisher's Acknowledgements

The publisher would like to thank Mike Rosel of the Australian Information Service, Melbourne and John Grigsby.

We must also thank the Australian Information Service, Canberra; Australian House & Garden Magazine, Sydney; BHP Co. Ltd, Melbourne; the Victorian College of the Arts School of Dance; Rip Curl Pty Ltd, Torquay, Victoria; the Sydney Opera House; Nomad Films International Pty Ltd, Melbourne; and Grundy Television Pty Ltd, Melbourne, for kindly supplying us with specific colour transparencies we requested.

Front cover: Jackaroo (Michael Coyne/Talentbank)
Back cover: Sydney Opera House (Ken Stepnell)
Front flap: Kookaburra (Ron Ryan, The Photo Agency, Melb.)
Title page: Country boy (Penny Tweedie/Talentbank)
Imprint: Country store (Ron Ryan, The Photo Agency, Melb.)
Acknowledgements: Fishing (Rennie Ellis, Scoopix)
Contents: Surfers Paradise (Ron Ryan, The Photo Agency, Melb.)

Contents

Meeting the People

In a sense life in Australia is too good to last. On the surface, most people appear well paid, comfortable and free from the class barriers found in Europe or Asia. But perhaps it is more like a game, an addictive game, than the serious business of survival in a ruthless world.

Many of us enjoy playing along with the rules. We sign away chunks of our earnings for years to come on hire purchase contracts, spend weekends at the beach and indulge our inclination for living with style; we are reassured by the cliche that ours is a classless society. But is it?

Beneath the surface, a sterner truth is waiting. The fact is that the wealthiest five per cent of the population owns more than the remaining ninety per cent. Furthermore, the five per cent is going to make sure things stay like this. In our so-called classless society there are in fact two classes: a large working class which lives by selling its labour (whether a person earns a basic $10 000 or a handsome $40 000 a year), and a middle class. Australia has no aristocracy. At the top of the middle class is a small faction of 'owners' — they own the mines, the media, the factories and the pastoral properties. The remainder of the middle class is a much more extensive group of people who vote for the Liberal and National Parties and would go down with the ship if it sank rather than admit they are really wage-earners with no power beyond the vote.

This broad, indeterminate band in the middle is interesting because it is made up of the people who represent the Australian dream of a fair share in the nation's wealth for everybody. They are the ones who take pride in announcing themselves as swinging voters. The greatest political upheaval since Federation (in 1901) occurred when a government came to power in 1972 with all the appearance of insisting that this illusion should be the reality. The owners were not going to let go without a fight. And to show where real power lay, they made the government's job almost impossible by ensuring that the legislation for change was blocked in the Senate, by withholding investment, and finally by having the government dismissed by the Queen's representative, the Governor-General.

To the chorus of 'C'mon Aussie C'mon' the crowds at the Melbourne Cricket Ground urge on their team.

Even now, more than a decade later and with the Labor Party back
in power, this crisis looms large in the Australian consciousness.
Who controls whom, whether we have a real say in our destiny are
questions that trouble us. This is particularly so now the economy
has been battered by recession.

The impression of a free-wheeling society on the move and
enjoying an all but guaranteed bright future was largely created in
the post-war years. An influx of migrants took over the lowest paid
jobs (in 1950 alone over 170 000 migrants arrived), and this allowed
the existing working class and children of the working class to rise
to white collar jobs, genuine comfort and a semblance of status.
Since 1970 this rise has virtually stopped. Now, just over a decade
later, we find ourselves at a turning-point, which just happens to
coincide with the computer revolution. No one can be certain what
will happen. It may be that the whole basis of production will be
stood on its head and the game-playing given a fresh lease of life.
Hence, the feeling is that we might equally well be on the edge of an
abyss, or about to launch into space.

Any visitor's first experience of Australians is likely to be the
workers in the street, people selling food or newspapers, driving
buses and repairing motors, people not wealthy enough to instal
themselves in private offices, not cushioned from the unexpected by
a hierarchy of clerks and secretaries. And perhaps this is as it should
be because, whatever Australianism might be, it is the creation of
working people.

Some nations take their tone and individuality from the
aristocracy, some (like Britain) from the merchant middle class.
Typical of colonists the world over, the immigrants here began by
preserving the accents of 'home'. Their descendants kept the
tradition. Even today, when the oldest pioneer families have been on
the land for six or seven generations, the worldly and fashionable

2

3

4

1   The Australian ethos has traditionally been male. But Australian women are remarkably free to express themselves, to achieve, to make their mark. The early female archetypes sprang from life in the outback where women battled beside their men to make a living from the bush. Two World Wars furthered the process: while men were away fighting, women took over their jobs. For the new generation of Australian women there is no going back. Nothing less than total equality is acceptable.

2   The punk influence on the Corso at Manly on Sydney's north shore.

3   Their detractors claim Australian women are unsophisticated and unfeminine. A fresh appraisal reveals, instead, a directness, unselfconsciousness and lack of guile as the hallmarks of emancipated womanhood.

4   A boutique in affluent Double Bay, Sydney, mirrors the latest trends in international fashion.

still prefer to identify with British traditions, Italian design, French flair and American vitality.

The alternative is doggedly Australian: the speech, the values and the manners of the workers, whose folk heroes are outlaws to a man, and whose uncouthness is as much encouraged by their peers as is the virility and knockabout stamina that often goes with it. The men are likely to see themselves as outgoing and casual, blokes who love their beer, who can handle a car and who are inclined to be a shade uneasy with the women. They may be foul-mouthed but they won't let you down when you need them.

The women have quite other ideas. Often enough they consider the men rather childlike in their simple pleasures (tinkering with engines and following sport) and altogether over fond of the booze. They see themselves as the intelligent ones, the money managers, the child-rearers.

The crowd in our city streets is such a mixed bunch these simplicities of self-image are seen to represent no more than a notion, a guess, a wish. Some people here have come from outback stock, with their nasal turn of speech that has taken generations of tight-lipped isolation to perfect, with their tweed clothing faintly redolent of livestock, their cheekbones and knuckles burnt by uncounted hours spent working in the open. Some people in the crowd are pale as aristocrats with gelatinous skin and Mendelssohn on the brain. Some are Asian, some African and South American. Many are from contending corners of Europe. Some are mixtures of these races so subtly blended their like cannot be found anywhere else. Whoever they are — in Sydney or Melbourne or Brisbane or Perth — they have a single expectancy in common, that this is a country where they have the right to be themselves.

They are a tolerant crowd who accept strangers willingly enough. The one thing that provokes antagonism is the sort of behaviour

2

3

1 Although the results are not always evident as yet, Australian men are beginning to slough off their beer-drinking sedentary image. Joggers and strollers in Melbourne's Treasury Gardens at Moomba Festival time are offered a distraction by the Herald Annual Outdoor Art Show.

2 Two of the characters at Paddington Market, Sydney. Every town and city has its markets and to browse through them tells much about the prevailing tastes and mood of the population. The wares range from tat and kitsch, to exquisite work in glass, clay, metal and fabric by skilled craftsmen and women, from memorabilia and antiques to old books, organically grown vegetables and naturopathic remedies.

3 Another perspective on the Australian male: a beach inspector, Sydney's Bondi Beach.

2

1 *Australia Day weekend and typically everyone flocks to the beach. Torquay, Victoria, packed to capacity.*

2 *Taking the sun, Western Australia.*

3 *A migrant woman enjoys the beach on her own terms.*

4 *Bliss and beauty on the beach.*

1 Queensland houses are regarded as 'quaint' by people living further south, but to Queenslanders they are simply a matter of functional good sense.

2 In contrast to the huge empty spaces of the interior, suburban Australia is singularly cheek-by-jowl. The Melbourne suburb of Templestowe is rapidly expanding. To foreigners the mysteries of 'brick veneer' are difficult to fathom: first a wooden framework is erected. Onto this goes the roof and only then is a 'skin' or veneer of brickwork applied.

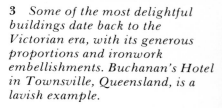

3

4

5

3 Some of the most delightful buildings date back to the Victorian era, with its generous proportions and ironwork embellishments. Buchanan's Hotel in Townsville, Queensland, is a lavish example.

4 Terrace houses in the Sydney suburb of Paddington were originally built to house workers. Today, those workers have moved further out into new homes, and this inner city suburb has become a very desirable address among people who compete for the pleasures of renovating sash windows, antiquated plumbing, leadlight glass and the like.

5 A man's home may well be his castle, but in the suburbs a swimming pool makes it a kingdom.

that used to be called 'putting on side'. To have exceptional ability, whether physical strength, intellect or imagination is one thing; to let it show is considered an affront.

Otherwise, anything goes — a casual jostle in pursuit of that paradise called 'lifestyle'.

Many in this crowd have left behind another existence in some distant country, a past of being shot at and insulted, of being ground down by centuries of fruitless labour, constantly looking over one shoulder for fear of being accused, caught, beaten up, conscripted. They have sacrificed a secure identity amid the customs and festivals of their forefathers. They are cast adrift from the language of their heart. English seems bodiless to them, a thin substitute for meanings that sing with history. They call out 'Okay Joe, lower away' from the top of building sites; they swelter in black dresses on Bondi Beach, marooned in the pulsing sensuality of naked-limbed locals (their own children among them); they weep over letters from their sisters still in nostalgic heartlands; they smoulder at insults from clerks and shop assistants. Yet they speak out bravely for the

1 *At the height of the 1982-83 drought Lake Eildon had shrunk to no more than a muddy stream. A year later, Bonnie Doon bridge in the background is once more just above the waterline.*

2 *Fire bears down on Lorne on 16 February 1983 — infamous Ash Wednesday. Earlier that day temperatures rose to 43 degrees Celsius and the land, aching from prolonged drought, was tinder dry. The stage was set for disaster.*

new country, they stand up and risk rebuff to say, 'This is my home, I am Australian now.' And why? Because there is something in the making here. There is a ferment, a possibility.

The cities are not finished — they never will be. It seems no sooner is a building up and graced with its first patina of exhaust soot than somebody is ripping it down to put up a bigger one. The skyline is almost as strange to old residents as to new. Ours are speculators' cities, a lottery of styles. Little is planned. In terms of architecture they have no single flavour like Paris or Peking, no consensus of good taste, like Budapest or Edinburgh. Yet each has its unique clutter of characteristics, distinctly its own and undeniably Australian.

More difficult than defining our cities is the matter of defining ourselves. Perhaps the unifying factor is no longer the idea of the archetypal Australian, but acceptance of the nation's complexity.

A decade ago we saw how joyfully the population rode the wave of nationalism that swept Gough Whitlam to power as Prime Minister. This was the new Australia. The new pride in being Australian didn't wait for analysis — it flooded through the streets in the most heady demonstrations of optimism in living memory. Although this enthusiasm was rudely checked in 1975 and has since been tempered by financial recession, the anguish of unemployment and the bitterness of admitting we are manipulated by overseas interests, it is still there, just below the surface. We glimpsed a brief flash in September 1983 when the country went crazy with America's Cup fever. I was among the 115 000 spectators at the Victorian Football League Grand Final who sent a concerted cheer via satellite to our yachtsmen at Newport, Rhode Island. Raw-throated and sentimental, we sang *Waltzing Matilda*. The unity of that colossal crowd and the twenty-four hours of jubilation following our victory over the Americans were events of contagious national excitement. Even for sceptics like myself who don't give a damn about yacht racing and deplore jingoism, sharing this much in common was irresistible.

There was never any hint of hesitation on the basis that yachting is a rich man's sport and football the 'people's game'. Yet, of course, there is an element of truth in this.

1 *In the grim aftermath of the Ash Wednesday fires, that characteristic Australian brand of humour showed through.*

2 *Not since Black Friday of 1939 had fire so ravaged Australia. Patio furniture and barbecue are all that remain of this home, destroyed by flames that at times raced more than a kilometre in a minute and a half, consuming everything as they went.*

3 *Cleaning up after the fire was a mammoth undertaking. The shock of this natural disaster reverberated across the world, which had shared the horror via the television screen. In Australia people rallied as one to the plight of the estimated 8000 left homeless.*

4 *United in sadness and loss, in courage and exhaustion, the fire-fighters and citizens of Upper Beaconsfield gathered for a service. In Victoria, more than 15 000 people had fought the blaze which killed 45 people, destroyed 1719 homes and left 330 000 hectares looking like the aftermath of a nuclear blast.*

5   *Symbol of life emerging from the ashes, a lily splashes pink after the first rains. Nine months after the fire, charred trees were cloaked in green, for the native vegetation is wonderfully adapted to fire, which has been a shaping factor in the Australian landscape for millennia. The people were slower to recover, but they too set about rebuilding their homes and their lives.*

3

4

5

Just how clearly footballers represent the local working people can still be seen in country towns where loyalties of place and family ramifications remain a living force. Friendships since school-days are commonplace. Locals share standing jokes, knowledge of the district. They have fought bushfires and floods together, they have survived drought and dust storms, plagues of pests. All these bonds are expressed most publicly at the sports ground where the crowds barrack for the local 'lions', 'tigers', 'raiders' or 'hawks'.

Guiseppe Stramandinoli is a handsome, muscular young man straight out of the Italian Renaissance, who has played Australian Rules Football for Queanbeyan, a New South Wales country town of about 20 000. He explains, 'The club is an essential part of the town. By that, I mean the supporters as well. Most of ours are probably related to some member of the team, but anybody can come and cheer and join in. We know them by their first names. They do important work like running chook raffles to raise money.

'Football is not just a sport. We identify with the town and the town identifies with us. We regard ourselves as the battlers and the underdogs. One of the coach's main cries is that we've got to do it for the town, the town's honour depends on us.'

This is true throughout the country for all codes of football, not just Australian Rules. Wynnum-Manly, for example, is an outer Brisbane suburban area with something of the coherence of a town in its own right. When in 1982 the Wynnum-Manly football team (Rugby League) won the Premiership for the first time in its history, the whole district declared a public holiday. Shops closed. People danced in the streets. Old man Fisher of Fisher's Hotel had provided for the possibility in his will, and accordingly the pub dispensed free beer all day to a throng of revellers. The celebrations lasted a week.

The big teams in Melbourne and Sydney have lost this intimate social role. The matches are theatrical events avidly watched on

1 *Near Derby, Western Australia, dried out mudflats make a first rate riding surface for local kids.*

2 *Montagu Downs, a cattle property on the edge of the Simpson Desert, sums up the isolation and unremitting harshness with which people in the outback must cope. Nearby permanent water makes it possible for the cattle and property owners to survive in this seemingly barren setting. The aeroplane serves as a vital link and people commute by air in the way suburbanites hop into the car. By the time they are old enough to drive, youngsters in the outback are seasoned pilots. Compared with urban Australia, childhood on the stations is hard. Many children are educated through the 'School of the Air', receiving daily lessons on a radio from a teacher who may be hundreds of kilometres away.*

television all over Australia: there are Collingwood and Parramatta supporters who have never set foot in either place. That close feeling of pride in the community, being part of an extended family, is gone. With players up for sale, huge contracts, and hard-sell advertising by sponsors, the game has turned into a commodity, merchandised like any other. This is not to say it has lost its appeal: the crowds are still there, the passions are rampant as ever, but it is no longer a symbol of belonging to a class and locality.

This same trend is apparent in city life. Of course, the impersonality grants a sense of freedom, people accept you at face value and privacy is respected. Even so, nostalgia for country values and the open-air life still haunts the crowds in Pitt Street and Swanston Street.

Out on the land there is space; space to live and move unhampered, space to ride, shoot, to create a little paradise, to be yourself or to go mad — above all, to face the physical challenge of survival. This is more a masculine than a feminine motivation so it is no surprise that the country is still populated largely by men

1 *August in Mt Isa, Queensland, and the Rotary Rodeo attracts rough riders from all over the state. The population almost doubles to 50 000 during the festivities as men and women test their skills.*

2 *Spectators at a Queensland rodeo.*

3 *Irrespective of the way they are, many Australian men see themselves in the mould of Slim Judge, seen here taking time off at the Normanton pub from his job as a shearer.*

4 *Often isolated, country women draw strength from opportunities to get together.*

2

3

4

(among rural workers eight out of every ten are male) where in all our main cities women are in the majority.

Who is this man on the land so many city dwellers carry round in their heads as a kind of talisman? He is physical — and this almost everybody admires — he is sun-browned and brawny. He works without walls and clocks. He is self-sufficient. His job is satisfying, he can see the beasts he rears or the crops he harvests. He is the epitome of independence.

This image is reinforced by television. Ironically, as average Australians become more sedentary, less physical, more in touch with events on the small screen than in the flesh, so they identify more strongly with 'the man in the bush'. Hat pulled low over his face, he is imagined to be like a man in a cigarette commercial, swinging himself into the driver's seat of a battered 'ute' and burning through the dust across impossible terrain to the limitless outback beyond. That is the image and it is a hat the city person feels he could well be wearing if only he could throw off his responsibilities, his debts, the habit of conforming. He sees himself on a horse, swatting flies the while. Or beside a campfire listening to his mates reminiscing — the tall story as an art form is alive and well in the bush — cigarettes glowing in the dark, the sweet smell of burning eucalyptus blending with the fragrance of hot tea from a black billy. Above all, the promise held out by life in the bush is a promise of being in touch with the soil. Sentimental it may often be, but this is what nags at many an Australian heart.

The reality of life in the country is pretty far removed from that. There is boredom, the grind, the appalling hardships of bad seasons, stronger social barriers between rich and poor, lack of diversity in entertainment, perhaps lack of entertainment altogether, loneliness, flies and more flies. Loneliness is especially severe for the women who are left at home on remote properties. Some women work with

1   *Living with any modicum of comfort at all in the bush demands ingenuity. This driller prospecting for minerals in the Kimberley carries his bath — complete with hot water system — wherever he goes.*

2   *When the drought of 1982/83 had finally withered every blade of grass on their land, this family gathered its remaining stock and took to the road. Responding to the hardship, the Pastoral Protection Board set aside areas in the Monaro-Kosciusko National Park in New South Wales and permitted stockmen to spend a night in each area before moving on in search of grazing.*

3   *Hamilton in outback Queensland appears on the map as a dot. But that dot is not a town; it simply marks the Hamilton Hotel where you can fuel your car, buy provisions, take a room for the night or have a long cool drink in the bar before facing the loneliness of the open road.*

2

3

the stock as jilleroos, many work the land with their husbands. But for most bush women isolation and boredom are real problems. Saddled with the responsibility for educating the children with the aid of a two-way radio and a teacher hundreds of kilometres away, often seeing little of her menfolk who arrive home late and dog-tired, she has more reason to be sceptical about this traditional promised land of the outback.

Yet many yearn for it, none-the-less, for its close family ties and deep friendships. A recent Gallup Poll showed that fifty per cent of all city dwellers would like to move to the country, but that only sixteen percent of country people would like to move to the city.

In keeping with this desire to remain in touch with the land, suburban gardens have undergone a transformation from neat English lawns with bright-flowered borders to native gardens of frail spiky blossoms and peeling bark. Barbecues are booming again — after all, they are a touch of outdoor living. And cars are driven as if there are great distances to be covered. Driving a car is regarded neither as a privilege nor as a convenience, but as a sovereign right. This attitude has a history. When the first automobile reliability trials were held from Sydney to Melbourne and back in 1905, newspapers across the country hailed the car as the bush people's saviour. Europeans and Americans might be fooled that these were extravagant mechanical toys for those who could afford them, but Australians recognised them as the solution to isolation.

The vehicles then, as now, were driven without mercy. Just about everybody who is of age drives, and drives with a careless rapture. We think as little of driving fifteen kilometres across town for the sake of buying a favourite gelato as we do a 1000 kilometre round trip interstate to attend an acquaintance's wedding, or even a party if it promises to be a good one.

Driving huge distances is normal in the bush. And it is partly

1   *The Chiko Roll — an Australian hybrid of the Chinese spring roll — takes equal billing with more familiar fare.*

2   *Any attempt to list Australia's 'national' dishes must include Pavlova — a sticky sweet dessert of meringue and cream topped with fruit.*

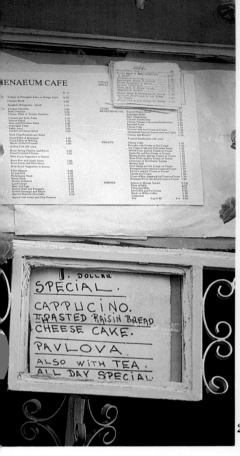

3   Components of the Australian cultural cliche: cork-festooned hat to keep off the blowies (flies), emblazoned T-shirt, and the ubiquitous 'pie and sauce'.

4   Sunday and the Yarra riverbanks are crowded with Melburnians disporting in the sort of setting that has earned Victoria the title of 'Garden State'.

because of this mobility that many of the smallest townships are dwindling and dying, as they are bypassed and cease to be essential supply centres. Most of the outback towns which have held on to their populations or have grown are mining centres.

Broken Hill in far western New South Wales is one of the largest of these communities. Each afternoon at three o'clock sharp the housewives of the town are reminded that far beneath them lie the tunnels of the lead and silver mines where their husbands work: right in the middle of the baby's resting time, the earth trembles, windows shudder in their frames until the day's blasting deep underground is completed.

For miners on the four o'clock shift, this is a useful alarm. I joined them one afternoon as they went to work. In the changing rooms and at the poppet head waiting for the lift, the most striking impression was of their spirit, the comradeship, the cheerfulness. Only twice have I experienced anything like it; once while a conscript in the army and once on a fishing trawler making ready to set sail, but the army was more competitive and the fishermen tended to work with the quiet methodical air of men with something on their minds. What these miners had in common with the fishermen was, perhaps, the knowledge of death. Each man ultimately depends on his mates for his safety. There is also a long tradition of pride in being miners. I stood in the lift with them, talking to the genial Operations Supervisor, John Gooding, who was taking me round.

The steel cage, a museum piece, dropped very fast, bucketing wildly against the shaft. More than a kilometre into the earth we travelled. The only light came from lamps on the men's helmets. One helmet I noticed had a sticker reading 'It's our mine, mate'.

Once down there at the stope, as they call it, the tunnel was thunderous with drilling and totally dark. During the moments

1   *The faces in the street portray the new Australian society.*

2   *When gold was discovered in Australia in the 1850s, trading in stocks and shares soon began and even what are now just provincial towns had their own stock exchanges.*

3   *A policeman comforts a little boy lost.*

4   *Mixed reactions among the crowds at the Melbourne Cup. Australians are a betting people whether it be the horses, the dogs or a flutter on the hugely popular lotteries.*

2

3

4

when the drilling stopped we could hear the wet darkness dripping into puddles at our feet. As the previous shift clocked off duty they exchanged a few words about the state of the job, and the quality of 'dirt' they had been moving. Some, they said, was probably sixty per cent pure lead. The other main news concerned a hot tip for the Saturday races.

In a mine like that, one is brought up against the knowledge that society runs twenty-four hours a day. It is easy to forget when you wake in the middle of the night and switch on the light, that but for the workmen at the power station the light would not work. Even our bread and milk supplies are taken for granted. But the bakers and milkmen (not to mention the dairy farmers) are up very early to prepare for the day's demand.

Keith Slater and his pastrycooks at Le Croissant patisserie in the Sydney suburb of Double Bay begin work at 3 a.m. They bake for the luxury trade, creations so delicate you would have to go to Paris to find anything as fine. Keith, a sturdy Australian, built to knead great wads of dough, runs an immaculate kitchen. He and his staff of three gyrate about the floor space, agile as gymnasts. Around them the mixers and blenders gently rotate. An all-night radio station churns out cheerful banalities: more people at work.

The patisserie is in an arcade and by the time the pastrycooks are into their home-run and the shop is due to open, the whole place begins to fill with women arriving for work, unlocking doors, preparing cash registers. There is a pleasant buzz of activity and conversation. Next, the office workers arrive, some calling in for a croissant as a late breakfast from a paper bag.

The phone rings in the patisserie. A woman in Parramatta orders $115 worth of pastries for a party. She will send a taxi in an hour. 'What's your fare going to set her back?' Keith asks as they load the car. 'Fifty-eight dollars at a guess,' the driver replies, 'She can afford

1 *Mini-cyclists, their adult seconds in close attendance, at a race in Canberra.*

2 *Broadly speaking, we are an undemonstrative lot, but the summer cricket season unleashes extraordinary passions. Newspapers headline the vagaries of each day's play and those who cannot take time off to watch the games, listen avidly to the radio.*

3 *Rugby is to New South Wales and Queensland what 'Footy' is to the people farther south.*

4 *Schoolboys from a private school. The State School system provides free education for all Australians, yet many parents who can afford the high fees choose to send their children to a private school. Criticised as being elitist, the private schools continue to prosper.*

2

4

it, she's always in the news.' The pastrycooks in the kitchen laugh delightedly. This is business.

Outside, the street has come to life. Double Bay exudes an air of success. This is a part of town where you seldom see a drunk or a derelict, an area in which the working class and the middle class confront each other daily in the course of business and trade. That this contact is usually amicable may means no more than that these are still good times for many of us. In addition, the working class has a special interest in seeing how the rest live, because that's where many of its members plan to end up themselves.

Perhaps the greatest promise Australia holds out is to the self-made man or woman. Compared with other countries, the chances of a breakthrough into comfortable wealth are remarkably attainable, and class interests are not nearly as entrenched. Those who achieve it seem quite ordinary really, not necessarily gifted with special powers or dynamic personalities. Many of the extremely rich are shy and even inarticulate in public; many retain their working class culture despite their income.

Our population is small enough for us to know who the millionaires are, and perhaps even to know somebody acquainted with them. Stories of how they began as penniless migrants or lone battlers are enthusiastically retold till they become public legends, precisely because people *want* such reassurances that the chances are there for them too. The hope is reinforced; all around they see evidence of newly expanding areas of work, business initiatives that offer room for those with ambition and flair, till their own success may seem but a step away.

1 *Midday and time for a 'smoko' in the glorious sun.*

2 *Affluence and disaffection in the suburbs.*

3 *Melbourne's Graffiti Wall was created as a focus for city wits and scribblers whose handiwork has liberally adorned the city.*

Faces in the News

Great success stories leave most Australians unimpressed. We do not look up to our successes the way other nations do. A secondary school girl began an essay on Shakespeare's tragedy with the claim: 'King Lear was an ordinary man and he had to face the ordinary family troubles with three daughters.' The divided kingdom, the wars of greed and the inner struggle against madness, the lofty language, the brutal torture, all were insufficient to dint that Aussie truism — I'm as good as anyone. So she proceeded to reduce Lear's grand collapse to a suburban squabble.

On the whole, the rich are not thought of as extraordinary people, but as ordinary people who have had extraordinary luck — or who have got away with something, as if they were swindlers, tax dodgers or at very least gamblers. Those among the rich who play this game skilfully are actually popular for having more loot than anyone else, for seeming to cock a snook at piousness.

'Our local member of parliament,' said a neighbour of mine who had been out of work for months, 'he's a great fellow, he never refuses to see you, you can call on him any time, he'll always listen to what you have to say.' No use pointing out that this parliamentarian's policies may well be responsible for aggravating unemployment in the first place. The common touch was a guarantee of goodwill.

In many cases Australians in the news themselves enjoy this earthy contact. They like to feel approachable, still in touch with the grassroots, while exercising the privileges of office. The most celebrated example is Johannes Bjelke-Petersen, Premier of Queensland. A peanut farmer, Joh, as he is called, has a rough manner and a blunt turn of phrase. He never refuses to be interviewed by the media and on every possible occasion reiterates his prejudices. He is always seen on the attack. He uses the simplistic terminology of a layman. Though he may well understand the complex forces of economics and politics, he is careful not to let this show. The popularity of his one-man-band government proves the continuing success of this image with the voters of Queensland.

Nothing, but nothing, like it had happened before. The national euphoria at winning the America's Cup transcended the race itself. It became a symbol of national unity that swept aside differences. It had all the ingredients of Aussie pride — taking on the giants, coming from behind, beating the odds through grit and determination. Perth, home of the winning yacht 'Australia II', turned out in force to fete its heroes.

1

The most successful political image today is that of the Prime Minister, Bob Hawke, who also depends heavily on his ordinariness. For years before he entered parliament, Hawke was one of the nation's best known faces. As an ambitious leader of the trade union movement, he was frequently on the front page. His pugnacious style and broad accent came across credibly on television. Occasionally he lost his temper and even abused reporters (which many viewers thoroughly enjoyed). And the moment he came to power as Prime Minister, the image was adjusted to suit his new responsibilities. Hawke's accent mellowed, his hair was cut, his volatile temper subsided to a frowning seriousness. But true to the Australian custom of hailing new leaders and then cutting them down to size, he has found himself caricatured in newspaper cartoons as no longer the people's man, but a little Caesar carrying a bust of himself wherever he goes.

Image-making in the media is controlled by very few. Every capital city newspaper and most provincial newspapers, nearly all commercial television stations and many commercial radio stations are owned by just four companies: John Fairfax and Sons Limited, News Limited, Australian Consolidated Press Limited, and the Herald and Weekly Times Group. All four have a great deal in common. They are in rivalry for money and power but not opposed to one another ideologically. They all present a business-oriented view of society and, in varying degrees, a right-wing view of politics. They also boast some of the greatest private wealth in the country.

Together they have immense power, power enough to win elections for the candidates of their choice; to create public self-awareness, or on the other hand to suppress news and destroy governments. Only the Australian Broadcasting Corporation stands apart as an independent news organization. This government-funded network was modelled on the British Broadcasting

1 *The team under skipper John Bertrand that broke the United States' 132-year-old grip on the America's Cup.*

2 *Rupert Murdoch, media mogul, with some of the newspapers that have made him such a formidable force. They have also helped make him, reputedly, the richest man in Australia. From a modest inheritance of the Adelaide 'News', he built his empire, first at home and then overseas where he has acquired such prestigious newspapers as Britain's 'The Times' and 'Sunday Times'. Turning his attention to the United States, he set off on a shopping spree that has so far*

included the Chicago 'Sun Times' (with a price tag of $90 million) and the New York 'Post'. His News Ltd is today the largest publisher of English language newspapers in the world, giving Murdoch unprecedented access to the minds of millions of people. His brash, sensationalist approach is criticised by many, but by the yardstick of money it is an unqualified success.

3   The $16-million mug and the jubilant Alan Bond who brought it home — and footed the bill. The 1986/87 America's Cup will be challenged on the rough waters off Western Australia, bringing a surge of tourism and world interest to Perth.

Corporation and has an impressive record for the quality of its programmes. The ABC has often been thought stuffy and bureaucratic in the past, but now it is undergoing a major reorganization by its new chairman, Kenneth Myer of the Myer Emporium family. And while its competitors in the news media become ever bigger and ever fewer (owing to take-overs) the ABC's impartiality, careful reporting and wide-ranging spectrum of topics, make it of inestimable value to viewers.

Richest and most powerful of Australia's press barons is Rupert Murdoch of News Limited. His family fortune has been estimated at a minimum of $250 million and his personal fortune at $135 million. He caused international sensations when he bought the New York *Post*, the Chicago *Sun-Times* and the most famous newspaper of them all, the London *Times*. To call his media holdings an empire is no exaggeration. Rupert Murdoch owns close to 100 newspapers on three continents, as well as the Channel Ten network in Australia. His other assets include an airline and an oil and gas exploration company. Murdoch, in this sense, is fairly

1   *Robert de Castella showing the form that has made him the top marathon runner in the world today.*

2   *The man who epitomises the word 'charisma' to the Australian public, Bob Hawke here in patriotic splendour in Perth for the winning of the America's Cup. After eight years in opposition, the Australian Labor Party's sweep back into power was as much a tribute to Hawke's ability to communicate with the people as it was to the prevailing mood for the change.*

2

3 Joh Bjelke-Petersen making friends Queensland-style. Premier since 1968, Bjelke-Petersen is essentially a conservative man of the soil, blunt-speaking and direct. The style of his leadership is perfectly attuned to the tastes of his electorate and his popularity in his home state continues to soar.

3

typical of the very rich in Australia and elsewhere — his companies are diversified and spread round various countries.

This movement towards internationalism and transnationalism is changing the world: businessmen come to see themselves as above and beyond politics, beyond even the interests of their native land, as if money and the making of money were an end in itself. The old concept of commercial rivalry is practically an anachronism, with a reshuffle of the same faces round so many board tables.

Another facet of this trend is being transmitted, I think, to Australians as a whole, with the media presenting less and less material of a kind to provoke and encourage people into thinking, into weighing up alternatives, into seeking national self-determination and national independence. The television and the press are powerful weapons in the neutralising of a nation's idiosyncrasies. They swamp the public with the violence, the sentimentality and the blandness of American programmes and dated Hollywood movies, in a process greatly strengthened by new television and video technology.

Kerry Packer of Consolidated Press is fascinated by technology, investing in the latest developments. His Channel Nine in Sydney is the world's first television station to be equipped with its own 'earth station' for receiving American programmes direct from the Intelsat Satellite. The system is fully operational but the government has yet to approve its use.

Although such technology could be used in Australia to bring television reception to even the remotest regions of the outback, its critics claim this kind of innovation might deal a further devastating blow to Australian independence of ideas and national identity. Fears that the United States of America will culturally, as well as economically, swallow us up grow more and more urgent. Already, with the limited quantity of satellite material screened on various channels, viewers find themselves watching parochial American items about storms in Florida or manhunts in Connecticut.

Mr Packer cheerfully admits newspaper proprietors are given to megalomania and includes himself. 'I believe I am far more enlightened than most of them,' he said in an interview for the magazine *Video Age*, 'but yes, I am quite capable of making a decision — maybe the term megalomania is too strong — to run something because I feel like it.' His company has expanded from a publishing operation into a conglomerate with sixty-three companies ranging over twelve separate industries, from mining to finance to video production.

In November 1983, the *Business Review Weekly* published a list of the hundred richest people in Australia (in fact it included 174 names). The article began by pointing out that 'The average value of the BRW One Hundred fortunes is $32.2 million, in a country where the average net personal wealth is about $28 000 and the average adult male income in the 1981-82 financial year was $9656. It is estimated that 1.5 million Australians live below the 'poverty line' established by Professor Ronald Henderson.' These, it must be emphasised, are personal fortunes, not company wealth, and they are only estimates at that.

One surprise is how few of these extremely successful money-makers are publicly known. Of course, the media and sporting personalities among them are household names, but the rest are rarely heard of outside the financial pages of newspapers. Another

1 *Australian sportsmen tend to be more newsworthy than politicians and Mark Richards is something of a celebrity, especially among the young. For the past several years he has dominated the international professional surfing scene, taking award after award.*

2 *Pat Cash, one of the young tennis players on whom our tennis hopes for the future rest. Since the days of Laver and Newcombe, our tennis showings have been on the decline but Australia's 1983 Davis Cup win may well have marked a turning-point.*

3 *Pam Burridge epitomises a certain Australian feminine ideal: fresh beauty and athleticism. In the 1982 season she ranked second in the world of women's surfing.*

1

2

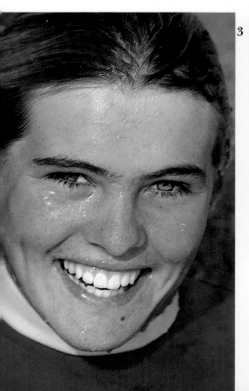

3

4

4   The mystique of beach and surf find perfect expression in the Iron Man contests. Like bronzed gladiators, their bodies honed to the peak of fitness, the young gods of surf lifesaving compete for the title. Grant Kenny successfully held the title for several years after his 1980 win. Combining all the surf lifesaving skills, the contest captures something of the ancient Greek ethos. On a more prosaic level, it is beginning to offer the commercial inducements that have transformed all fields of amateur sport.

remarkable feature is how their money was made. By far the largest group (twenty-five per cent) own fortunes made from property dealing and real estate. The next largest group (twelve-and-a-half per cent) made theirs from retailing. A mere five per cent derived their wealth from mining profits. The others range from financial services — a couple of merchant bankers, an insurance broker and an accountant — to the occasional millionaire sportsman.

But the really startling revelation is how few of Australia's private fortunes were earned from anything productive in the traditional sense of the world. We tend to think of pastoralists as the quintessential rich. But only ten of the 174 listed are primary producers (two being families of wine-makers). There are more race horse owner-trainers than beef cattle producers. The manufacturing fortunes are almost all in clothing.

Where are the industrialists, the owners of great factories and steelworks found in other countries? There is something insubstantial about our list: the timely resale of property on a market created by manipulation, and money making money.

To discern the effect of this money on the lifestyles of those who have it is difficult. As far as I can tell, they appear content with a more luxurious version of the suburban life the rest of us live. Doubtless, many quietly support charities and contribute to the costs of educational institutions; and there is still that remnant of the established squattocracy who live on their country properties and, culturally relating to their colonial traditions, fly direct to London if they need a taste of city life. But it still leaves the question: Where are the great entrepreneurial financiers, the Morgans, the Du Ponts, the Rockefellers of Australia? Where, apart from the Myer and Potter Foundation and three or four other small funds, are the private foundations? Where are the patrons of enlightenment and the avant garde? Alan Bond became a celebrity by spending grandly on building and racing yachts — his case is unusual.

With these sparse exceptions, the very rich appear to make little mark on Australian culture and, at least in public, contribute scarcely anything to the quality of life in the community.

One explanation is that a major part of Australian wealth is not reflected on a list such as this, for the simple reason that it is not in

1 *Dick Smith bedded down for the night beside his helicopter on the Meta Incognita Peninsula, Baffin Island. Drawn by the spirit of adventure, he became the first man to circumnavigate the world solo in a helicopter. The 30 000-kilometre trip earned him a string of 'firsts'. But he is more than simply a thrill-seeker; above all he is a successful businessman. His 'other' exploits smack of the spirit of the early explorers. He shares with them the imagination to expand the boundaries of experience and the guts to follow his inspiration.*

2 *Simon Crean, leader of the powerful Storemen and Packers' Union, outside the Trades Hall, Melbourne. The Unions have traditionally provided the power base for members of the Australian Labor Party. Hawke won his spurs here; Crean's time has yet to come, but while the entrenched party leadership discovers the pragmatism which government demands, a new generation of leaders is learning the vital skills of negotiation and power politics.*

2

3 Bob Ansett built his car rental business from a 20-car outfit in Melbourne. While he washed and serviced the cars, his secretary dealt with the public. That was in 1965. Today with over half the $150-million car rental business and a fleet of over 10 000 vehicles, Bob Ansett has his eye on air transport — not surprisingly in view of his father, Sir Reginald Ansett's empire-building in this area.

4 A 1984 survey of the 125 highest-paid Australians listed only one woman, Ita Buttrose. Composed and astute, she won the top post as editor of the 'Sunday Telegraph' and became a director of Rupert Murdoch's News Ltd, capping a career in which for many years she was editor of the 'Australian Women's Weekly', the largest circulation magazine in the country.

the country. A vast amount of our productive industry, mining and agriculture is not owned by Australians at all. These are areas dominated by the transnational combines. And it seems that successive governments, wittingly or not, have seen the marshalling of the nation's resources for the benefit of foreign interests as the best way to serve the national economy. They have become caught in a bind, based on the notion that nobody other than these giant corporations has sufficient capital and expertise to exploit Australia's resources, market them, and thus provide jobs and income to keep the financial system afloat. Whether this is so, and would have been so in the longer term, is debatable. Selling the orchard has often been the price we have paid for a rich and early harvest.

The balance a government strikes between the call for Australian ownership on one hand and community pressure for a style of life perhaps beyond our means on the other will hold the key to our future independence.

The question remains: What do these policies *mean*? What are the lasting social effects of decisions being made? Toughness and originality of mind are urgently needed in parliament. We are caught in the middle of world financial and political forces, the pressures are enormous. With our means of production so heavily owned and managed by foreigners, and our military defences almost entirely dependent on the United States of America, our room to manoeuvre independently and as we choose dwindles.

The decision to float the dollar, to deregulate exchange control, is a positive step in terms of the national economy. But it also clearly confirms our membership of the international business world. Nothing can cushion us from the rude shocks out there. In these days of jet aircraft, satellites and telecommunications, the surrounding seas are not the immense barrier they once were. Australia scarcely seems an island any more.

1   The Australian dream: a house, a job, a family. These three basic desires hold good for most Australians, but it is in their interpretation that much of the class system is based. Here a barrister, his wife and children frolic in their spa bath.

2   Often seen on the social pages, Sir Warwick and Lady Mary Fairfax entertain lavishly at their Double Bay mansion, Fairwater. Lady Mary is well-known as a patron of the arts.

3   To be an Australian today is to break new ground. Yet many cling to the old certainties, and the British colonial past is just one of these. Events such as cross-country riding hark back to these old associations.

The Land:
The Long Perspective

The biblical story of creation is said to have been written by Moses some 3200 years ago. There is no reason to suppose the Aborigines' sacred stories are any less ancient. And we should remember that on this same soil an Aboriginal contemporary of Moses could look back to an earlier story-teller equally remote; and from him to another before. Ten more times this immense history of belonging could be unfolded into the mystery of the past before reaching an age when we don't know whether or not human beings were in this land. It is, perhaps, the longest unbroken culture in the world.

Where did the Aborigines come from in the first place? No one can be sure. They themselves have no mythology of migration. Nothing in Aboriginal lore goes back to that remote age when people first came to inhabit Australia. They say they have always been here. But, of course, science demands connections, and various theories have been put forward.

The most generally accepted explanation is that the original arrivals came by a land bridge to the north during the last great Ice Age (which began about two million years ago and ended only ten thousand years ago). Ocean levels had fallen and this land bridge emerged, connecting the Malay peninsula to the chain of Indonesian islands, reaching almost to New Guinea which was then part of the Australian landmass. They might well have sailed across any intervening stretches by raft.

After this last ice age, world temperatures began to rise and polar ice caps shrank once more. The level of the ocean rose gradually but dramatically, cutting off all possibility of returning by land, and also preventing anyone else from following.

In India and the hilly regions of Malaysia, in the Philippines and Sri Lanka, there are still pockets of people with similar racial characteristics to the Aborigines. The difficulty of proving connections is complicated by the fact that the three identifiable racial types among Aborigines have interbred to produce a mixture not found anywhere else.

An Aboriginal man from Bathurst Island prepares for the week-long Groote Eylandt Festival. The pattern with which he so carefully adorns his face and body is not random. In the richly evolved myth and ritual of the Aboriginal people of Australia, body painting portrays many things — totems, symbols from the Eternal Dreamtime, or even a person's role or status on a particular religious occasion. The colouring, too, is traditional. The four colours — red, yellow, black and white — are derived from powdered clays, ochres, charcoal and manganese. These are mixed with substances such as orchid juice or egg to bind them for painting.

The most extraordinary thing is not these cold theories of race and origin but the cultural continuity for, in the Aboriginal view, some 40 000 years later, these two thousand generations of people still populate the land, the dead as well as the living. They *are* the land. Each tribe has an animal totem and each individual has a personal totem as well: the animals are their kin, often their spirit kin. Trees and plants may be spirits too. Forests teem with shadows — faces of the dead who may be recognised fleetingly by a descendant before a change of wind blows the leaves another way and the likeness is gone. The great ones among the ancestors lie on the land in magnificent panoply as mountains (sleeping, dying heroes yearning for the sea), as valleys of titanic footprints, as the stand of rocks where a council of elders took some momentous decision a thousand years before the Pharaohs dreamed of testing their geometry by building the pyramids.

The fact that these monuments are natural phenomena is what makes them miraculous: they have never been carved or otherwise tampered with by those who hold them sacred, never reshaped by human hand. This is the very quality that assures their sacredness, proves they were put there by divine power.

The difference between the Aborigines and the colonists was never more profound than in their inability to perceive what was sacred to each other. The fact that Aboriginal holy places were not man-made was the very reason the European mind could not (and still cannot) accept them as anything other than a category labelled Nature. Most probably Aborigines, for their part, dismissed Christianity as mere dabbling in magic because its shrines and symbols were so obviously the work of men.

Another basic difference was that Europeans looked on the land as a resource to be cultivated and quarried. By contrast, the Aborigines had never taken that critical step from use to abuse; they survived by attuning their society to the land as they found it. The only modification they were responsible for was accelerating the spread of grassland by selective burning. Tribes were distributed over the whole continent, some living along the fertile coastal plain, others far out in the desert, some in the cold Tasmanian mountains, some in the rainforest of the north. They were all hunter-gatherers.

1   *Pied geese east of Darwin.*

2   *A white egret sweeps towards its evening roost.*

3   *In a lily-studded pool in the far north, women hold up their catch of file snakes and freshwater tortoises.*

4   *The Northern Territory's magnificent Kakadu National Park has been leased to the nation by the Aboriginal people whose home it has traditionally been. Here a phalanx of pelicans glides along one of its rivers.*

5   *An immense saltwater crocodile basks at Yellow Waters in Kakadu National Park, safe from hunters but still threatened by companies keen to exploit the rich uranium deposits in the park.*

Following page: 1 *Escarpment country, Northern Territory.*

2   *Armed with her digging stick and an intimate knowledge of her environment accumulated by countless generations, a Pitjant-jatjara woman digs for witchety grubs — large insect larvae relished for their buttery flavour.*

3   *Bush tucker: berries together with a wealth of other indigenous plant foods have traditionally supplied at least half of the Aboriginal diet.*

4   *An Aboriginal burial site hidden deep in a cliff-face.*

2

3

4

5

1

2

3

4

Isolated stone structures have been discovered, including a village some 6000 years old (the exact site of which is being kept secret while archaeologists unearth it). Otherwise the Aborigines' shelters were temporary humpies and gunyahs — small tent-style structures of branches and leaves — or caves. This suited their mode of life, being the most efficient form of shelter among people who were nomads within their own territory, travelling established routes round it collecting food. And so they refined their skills of finding water and sustenance. Even the most forbidding areas were accessible to them.

A population of about quarter of a million appears to have remained fairly constant for at least 10 000 years, so their long-term management of resources was impressive. Moreover, the Aborigines appear to have controlled the birth rate efficiently. By means of a totem system which determined who could marry whom, many combinations of these symbolic animals were taboo, so the choice of possible partners was limited by a code as strong as the horror of incest. They ensured the bloodline remained vigorous whilst limiting the number of children. In these ways the Aborigines achieved a balance with the rest of nature and survived even in the harshest conditions, developing huge languages rich in idiom and nuance, religions of immense ritual complexity, and great traditions of art and dance, some of which have survived to the present day.

Each tribe was governed by councils of elders, men and women having different areas of influence. These councils interpreted the law. When the British arrived, they asked for the Chief. Having found there wasn't one, they corrected this state of affairs, chose a likely man and gave him a tin disc, with the name King Billy or King Jackie stamped on it to hang round his neck, and then proceeded to parley with him as an individual vested with power they acknowledged. The idea of communities voluntarily accepting ancient laws interpreted by a free association of elders appeared so unlikely they chose not to believe it.

Even more astonishing than the power structure of the tribes was that, until they were forced off their land into neighbouring territory, the Aborigines seem to have had no history of wars. Occasional skirmishes were fought. But these, according to pioneers such as Andrew Petrie who witnessed one, were conducted with a minimum of bloodshed, playing out ritual formalities which prevented matters getting out of hand. Nowhere in the country has a battlefield been dug up to reveal the bones of many dead.

The oldest human remains yet found in Australia were unearthed in the flat lands of outback New South Wales at Lake Mungo. The lake itself is dead, long since empty of water. It is possible to walk across the ten parched kilometres, from one bank to the other, to the clayey sandhills known as The Walls of China. Here, relics of the dune, compacted and almost rock-hard, have been worn by ceaseless winds. They stretch some fifteen kilometres, like ruined bastions and a rubble of towers.

Lake Mungo was part of an overflow system of the Lachlan River, once rich with fish, shellfish and birdlife. These, plus the marsupials that drank at the water's edge, were the game hunted by those tribespeople so long ago. Our evidence is in the middens, the 'kitchen waste'. Not only do modern carbon-dating techniques tell us this food was eaten some 38 000 years ago, but it is the earliest known case of shellfish as part of the human diet. The lake, so scientists believe, has been dry for at least 10 000 years.

1   *The Olgas, 32 kilometres to the west of Ayers Rock, spangled with a rainbow after a rare storm. Belief in the 'rainbow snake' is widespread in Aboriginal mythology.*

2   *Turkey Tolson, one of the Papunya Tula painters who live north-east of Alice Springs, with one of his works.*

3   *At Kintore, Uta Uta (in headscarf) works on a canvas for exhibition overseas. Modern materials give durability to works that belong to an ancient artistic tradition which Picasso once called the finest school of modern painting in the world.*

1

2

3

I stood in that wilderness of weather-worn towers, stung by flying sand, staring out across the lost lake, and found it hard to escape the feeling that this is like nowhere else on the face of the earth. More has been gouged out than remains. The emptiness is palpable, pervaded by the presence of what once must have been there; the foreshore just a relic rich with ghosts.

At the archaeological diggings the two human skeletons found so far, one man and one woman, are described in the terms of the profession as 'extremely gracile' — conjuring images of slender agile people. Somehow this gives the place the intimate quality of a graveyard. One would need to be cursed with a brutish lack of imagination not to feel grief for what white Australians have done to black.

In 1887 A. W. Howitt, who lived in this very area, collected and translated a song of the Woiworung tribe. The singer's name was Wenberi and the subject was his ancestors and his own mortality.

> We all go to the bones
> all of them shining white in the Dulur country.
> The noise of our father Bunjil
> rushing down singing inside this breast of mine.

Howitt recalled how, listening to the old man, 'I was moved almost to tears'. He went on: 'In the tribes with which I have aquaintance I find it a common belief that the songs, using the word in its widest meaning, as including all kinds of Aboriginal poetry, are obtained by the bards from the spirits of the deceased, usually their relatives, during sleep in dreams.'

Now, two centuries after the invasion, Aborigines are at long last being asked if they have any tales telling of their response then to the coming of whitemen. At James Cook University in Townsville, an oral history of Australia is being recorded. It appears that when the first Europeans arrived (the Portuguese in 1528 and the Dutch in

1 *Like a figure from Eternal Dreamtime, an Aboriginal child at the water's edge on Bathurst Island north of Darwin. The Eternal Dreamtime or Dreaming is common to all Australian Aboriginal religion: it reflects a melding of the real and spiritual worlds, of the conscious and unconscious elements of the human psyche. Its rituals seek to make real the myths and to bring harmony between man, his spirit and the outer world.*

2 *The shadow of a gum tree drifts above Aboriginal paintings in one of the 'art galleries' in Carnarvon Gorge, Queensland. Many of the larger rock shelters are adorned like this and littered with artefacts that attest to Aboriginal occupation in the past.*

1606) the tribespeople thought their ships were monsters, part-bird, part-fish. The men who landed were taken to be their own dead come back to life, because the dead were traditionally painted with white clay during the funeral rites.

After the colony of New South Wales was founded in 1788, sightings of ships along the coast became more frequent and the natives accepted that this had become an expected form of spirit behaviour. In some places people went down to inspect the sailors and, unable to recognise any as personal ancestors, drove them off thinking they must be spirits belonging to rival tribes. The 'spirits' then replied with loud bangs never heard before and made magic signs which caused warriors to drop dead without a single spear being thrown. In other places these returning spirits were recognised. They were greeted with the love and respect appropriate to dead fathers and husbands, they were offered gifts of their favourite food — whether grubs, moths, snake or meat — and given water. But then something else about them became apparent: their sufferings in the world of the dead had so shocked them they could

1 *The issues of Aboriginal rights — in more recent years specifically land rights — are still unresolved. The past two decades, however, have seen significant advances, partly as a result of the organisation of Aboriginal groups into effective political lobbies. Here a young man takes part in a demonstration in Sydney.*

2 *Seemingly bemused, a man outside Alice Springs' concrete-clad seat of justice.*

3 *Aboriginal rock paintings at Nourlangie, Northern Territory.*

4 *A different culture and different symbols. Sisters Rock in the Wimmera, Victoria.*

2

3

4

no longer remember anybody. They had forgotten every word of intelligible speech and could only communicate by signs, though they talked volubly among themselves in spirit-words.

Worse still, they had lost the art of social behaviour. They ate greedily and ignored the basic etiquette of sharing. After an initial show of relief at being kindly received, they often proved bad-tempered and bullying. They took women of totem groups forbidden to them, began cutting whole trees to build the biggest gunyahs ever seen and shut themselves away inside.

Meanwhile, more arrivals from the sea brought huge animals, fabled beasts with feet hard as stone and long spikes growing from their heads. They uttered terrifying bellowing noises and were as belligerent as their owners. More dangerous still, the spirits brought a woolly animal the size of a wallaby, a calm and silly creature evidently sacred because if ever one was speared for its delicious meat, the white spirits came chasing the tribe, letting off bangs and murdering people in revenge.

Even when these ghosts were friendly, the outcome could prove fatal. Sometimes, after contact, whole families would break out in spots and fire would rage in their blood till they died.

Eventually, the truth dawned on the people of Australia, people who had been undisturbed for tens of thousands of years: they were not the only humans in existence, their land not the only land. Out beyond the sea must be other countries where these unwelcome visitors belonged. The white men were men, not spirits after all. They were not ancestors, they had no right to be here. What was most unthinkable, unimaginable, was that they had come to a land not their own with the intention of staying.

The newcomers fenced sacred waterholes. Robbed of their water and the grasslands they had encouraged for their game, the people found themselves driven into other tribes' territories. Wars began

Previous page   Toby Kaninga and his tribe have lived near Ayers Rock for thousands of years. Now it is theirs again. In 1983 the government gave title to the Uluru National Park (in which the rock stands) back to the half-dozen Aboriginal families whose home it has always been. Spiritual and physical heart of the continent, this imposing monolith is not only of significance to Aboriginal Australians. Each year it receives a constant flow of visitors — many of them urban Australians for whom a trip to Ayers Rock has taken on overtones of pilgrimage. The 335-metre weather-worn rock is all that is visible of a larger rock turned on its side by ancient geological forces.

2

3

1 Ever since Europeans set foot in Australia, change has been inevitable among the Aboriginal people of Australia. With contact has come Western technology, urban living and an entirely different economy. But this change has come at a price. The values and social fabric that gave identity and strength to people such as these old men at Ayers Rock have been eroded.

2 Weather-sculpted sandstone cliffs at Point Leveque, Western Australia.

3 Devil's Marbles, near Tennant Creek, Northern Territory, are weathered granite. Several Aboriginal legends are linked to them.

where there had been peace before. The whitemen set about systematically chopping down the forests, clearing away the shades of the ancestors as they went. Even the great heroes were sometimes destroyed when the tops of mountains were blasted and gouged away or buried under a sprawl of houses. The tribes hit back.

Once they realised what was happening, they fought. From all over came reports of small-scale battles and bloodshed. A few at a time, the people were defeated: ten shot here, a dozen poisoned there, disease taking half a clan somewhere else. Then came a most unexpected enemy — gangs of traitor Aborigines dressed in whiteman's clothes, armed with whiteman's weapons, using traditional skills of tracking and survival. These agents of the alien rampaged across the boundary of family sanctuary, shooting and terrorising the people.

Valley by valley, the tribal lands were lost and transformed beyond recognition. The invaders were achieving the impossible — taking the whole country and turning it into a replica of the lands from which they had come.

1 *Spinifex — so typical of the Australian outback — its taut, rounded tussocks studding the countryside. Spinifex is marvellously adapted to the rigours of the climate and provides food for stock even in the most unforgiving drought. Traditionally, the Aboriginal people extracted its resin as a gum to bind items together.*

2

3

2　*Backed by choking dust and smoke from a bushfire nearby, a desert oak endures in Central Australia where temperatures often soar above 40 degrees Celsius and rainfall is scant.*

3　*Acacia seedpods, Western Australia.*

The Black Wars, which reached their critical phase in the 1840s, were still being waged in Queensland and Western Australia twenty years later. Elsewhere the greed engendered by the goldrushes had finally sealed the defeat of the original inhabitants. Some, of course, have never stopped the struggle against being taken over, and violate the imposed social order whenever possible. Among them are people who still believe they will one day re-inherit their homeland (much as the Israelis have); that the white people will go.

The British, when they took formal possession in 1788, had no knowledge that this was anything more than a country of fine harbours and unique wildlife. They were not to know that tribal territories spread over the entire area of the continent, with all its extremes of climate and its variations of vegetation, that wherever they landed they would displace people, causing shockwaves of tribal conflict. The war was never declared nor any treaty signed.

For a hundred years the Aborigines were considered subhuman, shot for sport by hunting parties of colonists, or re-educated by missionaries who undermined their faith in the spirits. Though they fought fiercely, they failed to stem the invasion. This failure is usually explained in terms of the British having superior fire-power. But the flintlock weapons of the time, though frighteningly noisy, were slow to load and inaccurate. A more significant reason might be that the Aborigines had no tradition of warfare, no concept of banding together in the face of a common enemy. The idea of an army was unknown to them and their resistance remained disorganised.

By 1850 the invaders outnumbered the natives. The whiteman was here to stay. Modern Australia had been born.

1 *In the public imagination the kangaroo is synonymous with Australia — and with some justification for it is confined to this continent and is widespread. Controversy rages today on the subject of culling. Some argue that it may endanger certain species of kangaroo. Farmers, on the other hand, claim that the kangaroo population has become so large it threatens their livelihood and that the animal should be regarded as a pest. At present, kangaroos are widely culled on a fixed quota basis, their meat being processed, mainly as pet food.*

2 *With vivid blooms up to ten centimetres long, Sturts Desert Pea bejewels Australia's often drab inland areas.*

1

2

3

3 *In a country renowned for its glorious parrots and cockatoos, Australians tend to take the galah for granted. Perhaps this is because it is so common both in the countryside and in built-up areas where this gregarious rosy-breasted parrot with its unmistakable high-pitched 'chill chill' and harsh screeching has found a congenial existence.*

The Land:
A Wealth of Resources

Captain James Cook sailed away from Australia in 1770 with little idea of what he had found. He set the Union Jack in the soil and left it there, a laughably frail gesture, fluttering in the same wind that sent him scudding home. The land bearing that flag seethed with activity. Later descriptions of emptiness took no account of what was already there, only of what was expected.

Europeans still had hopes of finding the kingdom of Prester John, a legendary Christian king, immensely powerful and pious. This was the court Marco Polo thought he had discovered in China, the earthly paradise Columbus expected in the Indies. Since at least the fifth century BC they had speculated about a Great South Land (which is what 'Australia' means), but they visualised lakeside palaces, princes hunting on horseback while docile slaves dug gold for the greater glory of the Church or court. And many parts of Asia and South America had brought them fabulous riches in gold, in spices and in silk.

Most early European trade with the Far East was by ship, so safe ports along the way were crucial for success. The Dutch had their harbour at Batavia (Jakarta); the Portuguese had the island of Timor. France and Britain, in order to hold and expand their share of the spoils, had to find more ports in the area. In 1785, the French sent Jean de Galaup, Comte de la Perouse, to investigate the South Pacific for harbour sites and this prompted the British to act on the recommendations made fifteen years earlier by Captain Cook.

Cook had been commissioned to find a suitable harbour in the region. He was sent under cover of a scientific expedition to observe the planet Venus in transit between Earth and the sun (a phenomenon only visible in the southern hemisphere). So began the first stage of colonisation of the 'Great South Land'. After a voyage notable for Cook's brilliant navigation and management of his crew's welfare, he had returned with news of a harbour at Botany Bay. So a decade and a half later, men and supplies were dispatched to set up a colony there, with an unpaid workforce in the form of convicts from England's overcrowded gaols.

Under the command of Captain Arthur Phillip they arrived in January 1788, and waded up a low-lying marshy shore. Six days later

Ghost gums, elegant against this steep rockface in the Ross River area of the Northern Territory. Much of the Australian landscape takes its distinctive character from the more than 600 species of eucalypt or, as they are more commonly called, gum trees. They range from the soaring karri, almost 90 metres in height, to shrublike species a metre tall. Now that the huge plantations of fast-growing imported tree species have begun to reach maturity, pressure has been taken off the indigenous hardwoods. Many Australian trees have adapted to survive onslaughts by fire and drought but are often extremely slow-growing.

on 26 January — now celebrated as Australia Day — Phillip decided to establish the port at a superior site, Sydney Cove. A day later, La Perouse sailed into Botany Bay to find it occupied.

The new arrivals were observed by Aborigines, some of whom came out boldly to meet them; some, crusted with clay and stuck with leaves, slipped away unseen into the bush. Curiously enough, seven years were to pass before the first major clash between Aborigines and colonists. But the land itself proved harsh. Governor Phillip's garrison suffered appalling privation. Soldiers, convicts and the governor himself lived close to starvation for two years, until the first ships from England arrived, carrying not only supplies but more mouths to feed as well. During that time, it does not seem to have occurred to this usually sensible gentleman to ask the Aborigines, who were obviously healthy and well-fed, for advice on which indigenous plants were edible and on how to hunt the wild animals.

Gradually the crisis passed. One by one the farming projects began to yield crops. To help consolidate the port of Sydney, Phillip gave 30-acre (twelve-hectare) grants of land to marines and to convicts released for good behaviour. This policy not only assured future supplies, but persuaded men that there were prospects here, that it was worth staying beyond the term required of them. Under this simple patriarchal system a class of owner farmers emerged.

Governor Phillip's successor, Major Grose, disturbed the colony's stability by handing out much larger holdings, this time not to labourers but to officers of the New South Wales Corps. Provided with salaries and ten servants apiece at the public expense, they raised loans from regimental funds, money from their families in England and Scotland, and embraced the concept of anarchy among those who could afford to ignore authority. This trend still has its followers.

1   *Tourists at the Penny Royal Gunpowder Mills, Launceston, Tasmania. Launceston was begun in 1806, three years after 'Hobart Town' was established in Van Diemen's Land (as Tasmania was then called) on instruction from the Governor of New South Wales. From the start, the population of Van Diemen's Land was largely convict and even fifteen years later, convicts far outnumbered free settlers.*

2   *Port Arthur, Tasmania, cloaked in sylvan grace that belies its past as the most infamous penal settlement in Australia. Today the beautiful convict-built church and buildings are a historic reserve.*

3   *The paddle steamer 'Melbourne' on the Murray River near Mildura, Victoria, evokes an earlier era when boats such as this on the Murray-Darling river system opened up much of New South Wales, Victoria and South Australia.*

2

3

By 1795, farms had spread out along the Hawkesbury River, some seventy kilometres north of Sydney, and 500 people lived in the district, apparently feeling themselves sufficiently remote from the law to indulge in riotous behaviour.

Here, too, they fought the first pitched battle against Aborigines who, they claimed, were interfering with the 'peaceable possession' of the land. Victory endorsed their determination to stay.

The land, particularly along the well-watered eastern seaboard, was highly desirable. Much further inland stretched the formidable wastes of the centre. And so, as has happened wherever Europeans set up colonies around the world, there was friction with the native population over resources. At first it was over water, game and timber, later over land for wheat and sheep. Where Aborigines may have held a forest sacred, a hill to be of ritual significance, a creek part of the spiritual life of their tribe, the whiteman could see only profit. But above all both needed the land to survive.

The most valuable products of New South Wales in those early years were provided by timber-getters who cut logs for ship-building and repair, by whalers and by seal-hunters. As early as 1799 the *Martha* carried a shipment of 1300 sealskins and thirty casks of seal oil to England. Grain farming had also begun showing signs of success, especially in the capable hands of James Ruse, the first freed convict to be granted land. And merino sheep, originally imported from the Cape of Good Hope in 1797, flourished.

Even in these infant years the patterns of Australian wealth were becoming established: on one hand the import-export market; on the other, profits from growing wheat and keeping sheep. Petty corruption became the rule.

During the six month period ending in May 1800, the extraordinary volume of 36 000 gallons (162 000 litres) of spirits came into the colony — at that time consisting of a mere 5000 souls.

1, 3   Boom and bust stories are a common phenomenon in the Australian past. So often grand dreams foundered when the promise of even bigger profits beckoned. Silverton, in the far west of New South Wales, conforms to this pattern. The gaunt building (3) and silent Roman Catholic Church (1) recall the 1880s when silver and lead were discovered here. When even better finds were reported from nearby Broken Hill, Silverton was abandoned.

1

2

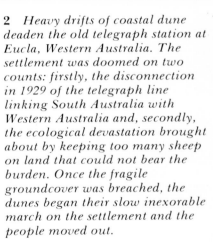

3

2 *Heavy drifts of coastal dune deaden the old telegraph station at Eucla, Western Australia. The settlement was doomed on two counts: firstly, the disconnection in 1929 of the telegraph line linking South Australia with Western Australia and, secondly, the ecological devastation brought about by keeping too many sheep on land that could not bear the burden. Once the fragile groundcover was breached, the dunes began their slow inexorable march on the settlement and the people moved out.*

1 Wielding his 'comb' with what appears to be no more effort than one would need to shrug off an overcoat, a shearer removes the hefty fleece from a sheep.

2 Shearers taking a rest from their backbreaking work.

3 Mustering by motorcycle on parched Maghera Station west of Bourke, New South Wales. The wool industry soon transformed Australia from a dumping ground for convicts into a legitimate and wealthy member of the British Empire. Although sheep were part of the survival kit brought out by the first settlers in 1788, it was only with the introduction of the thick-fleeced Merino just over ten

3

4

years later that the wool industry was born. Wool soon became the mainstay of the Australian economy — even with the vagaries of the world market and the later competition from synthetics. Today, though no longer the greatest source of wealth in this country, wool is still a major export earner.

4 *A far cry from the early days on the sheep stations: man, motorcycle and friends.*

In terms of political sophistication, a warning for the future might be found in Governor King's solution to the evils of the 'Rum Trade'. That same year, 1800, he requested the transportation of two Frenchmen, prisoners of war who had been in Napoleon's army. They were to advise him on developing the Australian wine industry which had its modest beginnings at the time of the First Fleet. As a result, a year and a half later, King had 18 000 vine cuttings brought in and planted. Hops and brewing equipment were also ordered and official beer production began at Parramatta in 1804. The effects of this wine and beer did nothing to alleviate the problem.

The self-interest of the rich was notorious — to the extent that they openly opposed those governors who would not comply with their dictates. They set themselves against any appointee who had firm intentions of actually governing the colony. With the help of powerful connections 'at home', they broke the authority of Captain William Bligh and Lachlan Macquarie, both strong-willed men with a belief in their public mission to govern the colony.

For the next half century the pattern was set. The officers, free settlers and even a few freed convicts 'squatted' on vast tracts of what was now called Crown Land, which is to say they occupied it without permission and raised their sheep there. In both New South Wales and Tasmania they assumed the airs of aristocrats, built themselves country mansions and set about establishing dynasties.

The poorer folk, who remained near Sydney or Hobart, found conditions more difficult. Unable to simulate the comforts of the old country, they lived more directly in touch with the reality of being aliens. Their towns were a huddle of modest buildings perched on the edge of an immense unknown hinterland which had nothing in common with anything they had known. But the climate was magnificent; they even thought this in cold Hobart. The vegetation which they might have expected to be as colourful as the jungles of Asia or Africa, appeared to their eyes scrawny and drab, the subtle vocabulary of greys and greens too muted to appeal to memories of English fields and beech forests brilliant with spring. From the first, they were not looking for the new, they were looking for the familiar; they did not want to be here at all. So, once they decided to colonise this outlandish place, with an energy as astounding as their blindness to its native beauty, they set about converting it to a likeness of the British Isles.

A single word gives the clue to how they saw themselves and what they believed they were doing: they called the invasion 'settlement'. And 'settlement' is a peaceful process which implies no prior ownership. With single-minded determination most people refused to acknowledge the war of occupation for what it was. When 'settlers' went into new territory they went armed, that's all, and sometimes they had the misfortune to be forced into defending themselves. But, like colonists everywhere, they never acknowledged the status of those against whom they defended themselves.

The reconnaissance for these incursions was financed officially and carried out by explorers. Once again, the choice of word has importance. To these British explorers was attributed the 'discovery' of the land. That every hectare was already known in all its facets by the people who already lived there was conveniently ignored because, by definition, to 'discover' a land is almost to bring it into being. Interestingly, these words with their misleading eloquence are still being used.

1 *Rotors, heavy tyres and surging cattle in the Kimberley, Western Australia. Beef cattle have always been an important part of the Australian export economy. They thrive in areas where the extremes of heat and cold are less pronounced. Because of the often sparse nature of the Australian outback, cattle properties there tend to be immense, although the number of cattle sustained per acre is contrastingly low.*

2 *Branding heifers on a property in the Northern Territory. Life on the outback properties is hard, isolated and, when the elements are unforgiving, bankrupting. Yet many of the Australian archetypes spring from these parts: men and women whose very core seems tempered into steel and whose independence is much admired.*

1

2

The explorers were all men. But that is about the only thing they had in common. Some, like Lt Flinders and Dr Bass, explored by sea. Most set out by land to map the interior. They were a mixed bunch: aristocrats and ex-convicts, young and old, experienced and green, naval officers, doctors, graziers, surveyors, policemen and soldiers. A few set off purely for the sake of adventure or to bring honour to their name. Most were encouraged by promised rewards for finding pastoral lands, gold or large waterways. The merchants who backed them when the Governor did not, remained safely in town, fretting over the money they had risked. Some explorers were inspired to superhuman efforts by visions of glory, others by the previous failure of their lives. Some went with a bare minimum for survival, others like Burke and Wills took cumbersome quantities of equipment such as an amphibious wagon and leather shoes for the camels. Many did not survive.

The famous stories of the day were feats of endurance. In 1795 Bass and Flinders survived the open sea in their eight-foot boat *Tom Thumb*. In 1840-41 Edward John Eyre trekked overland from Adelaide to Perth with one white companion and three Aborigines. They set off into the desert in late summer: not a wise decision. He and one of the Aborigines, Wylie, survived, and became a sensation. Two new names were entered on the lists of colonial heroes.

Equally celebrated were the tragedies. Burke and Wills died on their way back from a south to north crossing of the continent. Ludwig Leichhardt and his entire party of seven men, animals and equipment vanished without trace beyond Cooper's Creek in central Australia in 1848.

The drama lay in the risks they took and the gamble of their backers. Whether victims of treachery or darlings of luck, they were beyond the hatred festering between the greedy and the deprived, free citizen and convict. The whole community was fired by the thought

1 *A buffalo catcher and his dog relax after the chase. Although buffalo are a fairly common sight at the Top End of Australia, they are not indigenous. Brought from Indonesia at the end of the 19th century and later set free when various settlements were abandoned, these massive bovines now support a profitable meat industry. The catchers muster them, using helicopters and rugged four-wheel-drive vehicles. Most of the meat is exported.*

2 *A fortune on the hoof, beef cattle on the Tully River Ranch in northern Queensland.*

of them out there, dying in an attempt to reach a promised land of fertile plains around an inland sea long since dried to dust.

In the wake of the explorers came pioneers, pushing through virgin scrub, over seemingly endless ridges, lured on by great expectations. They left the nation a legacy of stubborn independence, a refusal to knuckle under. They carved pastures out of dense scrub. Each family fenced a run, built a shack and graced it with the name 'the homestead'. They survived this land's catastrophic fires, droughts and floods. And, as if the struggle against the land were not enough, they then had to contend with slumped markets. Many pioneers lost everything for which they had worked so hard. But those who stuck it out and reared their children in the bush founded a new breed. The countryman became the quintessential Australian: tough, laconic and resourceful. This image — his and his wife's — distinguished the Australian as a type, with far distances in their eyes, and scorn for those in authority.

That was how Australians saw themselves; and that was how they began to be. The fact that they were often brutal and ignorant, given to whingeing and grumbling, was no part of this ideal. The clearer the image the more accepted it became — and no one clarified it more memorably than the anonymous bush-balladists. The woman in *The Banks of the Condamine* comes to mind as a fine example. She plans to share the hardships of a shearer's life and sings:

O Willy, dearest Willy, O let me go with you.
I'll cut off all my auburn fringe and be a shearer too.

When Willy claims she would not be able to 'withstand the constant tigering' on the banks of the Condamine River, she persists:

O Willy, dearest Willy, then stay at home with me;
We'll take up a selection, and a farmer's wife I'll be.
I'll help you husk the corn, love, and cook your meals so fine
You'll forget the ram-stag mutton on the banks of the
Condamine.

1 *Hulking mechanical harvesters such as this one working a Glencoe property near Wee Waa, New South Wales, bring in the mammoth sugar harvest. Not only does this fully sweeten the home market, but places Australia third to Cuba and Brazil as a world exporter of sugar.*

2 *Australia's cotton harvest is largely destined for the domestic market.*

3 *It seemed as if nature, having tested the endurance of farmers with three cruel years of drought from 1980 to 1983, now turned a smiling face. The new rains transformed the Australian wheatlands' dustbowl conditions into a rippling cloak of ripening grain and the combine harvesters were out in force bringing in the biggest Australian wheat harvest ever. Once more income from wheat soared to first place in earnings from agricultural produce. Only three per cent of the world's wheat comes from Australia, but because she exports 80 per cent of her total crop, her international role is significant.*

The pioneers thought of the land simply and optimistically as property to be reshaped. By a combination of hard work and luck they believed it would provide first a subsistence and then a profit.

In Melbourne and Sydney, average citizens then were much like they are now, in one respect at least: few ventured beyond the safe limits of their settled life, but all felt an intimate awareness of that great dry land waiting out there, just beyond the rim of their experience. Yet, even in the safe familiarity of urban life they identified with the pioneers as ordinary folk fulfilling ordinary folks' dreams. The wealthy did not avoid a touch of this too, though they aimed to preserve the accent and manners of their British origins.

The explorers, by contrast, were far from ordinary. They were exceptional individuals who, even after the time when gold was discovered, remained legends in the colony. Gold changed just about everything else.

In present-day values, the gold mined in Australia during the nineteenth century sold for about $50 000 million. The population, during the 1850s alone, trebled. Large areas were reduced to wasteland, stripped of all vegetation, dug up and left as barren heaps of mullock. The gold seekers' motto seemed to have two propositions: if it is there, get it out and sell it fast; when it is all gone, get out yourself and don't look back. Until the 1960s when the conservation movement began to take hold in the public imagination, mining companies of all kinds continued to operate on this basis.

Boom towns boasted flamboyant public buildings among the shacks and grog shops. Railway lines were laid to connect them with their respective capital cities and the coast. Roads were put through. But while the concept of a nation, as distinct from a hinterland, had begun to emerge, the gold boom revealed all the weaknesses of any

1 *Opening a lock on an irrigation channel near Griffith in the important Murrumbidgee irrigation area of New South Wales. Australia is the driest of the continents and, even in areas of adequate total rainfall, seasonal fluctuations make farming difficult — if not impossible. Several immense irrigation schemes have greatly increased the area under crops.*

2 *A picker savours grapes from this New South Wales vineyard. Australians are drinking more wine than ever and new varieties are continually being developed. The industry, however, is not new: the early settlers brought out cuttings and planted them near Sydney. Since then both quantity and quality have improved. Today there are vineyards in all of the States and the Territories, but South Australia has probably produced some of the best known Australian wines. Recently, in open international competition, wines from estates such as Rosemount and Tyrrell's have taken top awards that traditionally go to the famous French and German makes.*

society financed by money from mining. There was no planning for the future or for when reserves might run out. At the height of productivity in 1899, Charters Towers in Queensland was known locally as 'The World'. Boasts and outrageous claims to notoriety were common, typical of a gold town. A decade later the place was in decline. Now there is no gold worth mining there at all. It seems that these trends and attitudes, when it comes to natural resources, are as prevalent as before.

Throughout the country, when all the easy pickings had been claimed and the few had become rich, mechanised mining took over. The day of the individual digger was past and tens of thousands of them stayed in Australia rather than face the failure and expense of returning home. They were the new labour force.

Impermanence has marked so many Australian enterprises. For a young society, the landscape is astonishingly littered with rusted relics of machinery and crumbling, abandoned towns. The hunger for short-term advantage, whether in mining or agriculture, timber-getting or water usage, has left Australia with complex problems. Time and again the balance between land and land-use has been upset on a large scale. The irony is that each collapse of an industry is greeted as a stroke of bad luck. No one ever seems prepared. That public relations word 'settlement' suggests a promise of permanence we take for granted; experience should warn us otherwise.

In the same manner the cedar forests of Queensland were wiped out to satisfy a ready market. This native species is now extinct.

Indiscriminate clearing of forests and bush for agriculture has led to salinity problems in the soil. Without the roots of trees to control the water deep in the soil, the water-table has risen, bringing salts to the surface. Here evaporation leads to a concentrated deposit that poisons all plants.

Stripped of its protective layer of vegetation, the land is now open to the ravages of wind and water and becomes irrevocably eroded. Similar lethal effects can occur where irrigation schemes (such as the Murray River irrigation scheme) release dammed water and cause the natural water levels to rise in the soils, once more bringing salt to the surface.

The Heytesbury Scheme is a recent example of salination through the widespread removal of the natural vegetation. This dairying project was set up north of the Otway Ranges in Victoria after the Second World War. The farmers continued to clear the forests until 1972, but rising salinity levels eventually made the soil unworkable. Ironically, these problems were understood and solved by the ancient Mesopotamians, yet we still wrestle with them.

None of the animals raised for meat, wool or as working beasts, is native to Australia. Our entire food production — except for the macadamia nut — has been a case of transplantation of exotic species. Small wonder some ran wild.

The fact that no indigenous animal has hoofs may not appear significant, but the effect of the hooves of hundred-millions of sheep, cattle, horses, pigs, goats, donkeys and camels has been devastating on plants and soil-types which never had to withstand this sort of punishment before.

The rabbit, usually named as villain in the story of denuded land, has probably done no worse damage than the sheep. But its effects are none-the-less terrible. Rabbits came with the First Fleet in 1788. Others were introduced at all the main population centres for the

1 Hop fields with their elegant rows of sheltering poplars at Eurobin, Victoria. Beer, brewed from hops, is the national drink — our consumption is up with the Germans and the British in the world's top five. Most hops are grown in Tasmania.

2 Arabesques of lavender in flower on a commercial lavender farm in Tasmania. The delicate fragrance from this plant is distilled into essential oil and exported. Tasmanian lavender accounts for 15 per cent of the world's supply and is mostly used in the perfume and cosmetic industries.

1

2

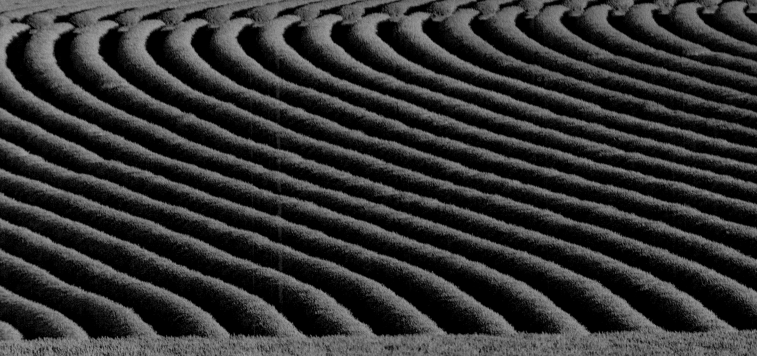

next seventy years, but showed no sign of breeding fast enough to become a problem. Then in 1859 the clipper *Lightning* arrived with a consignment of wild rabbits from England for Thomas Austin of Barwon Park near Geelong, Victoria. He let them loose and within three years they were declared a pest. Australia's vast rabbit population is thought to have developed from this stock.

Dramatic scenes of a losing environmental battle can be seen at Eucla on the border of Western Australia and South Australia. This little town, set up at the coast as a telegraph station, was busy and thriving for a while. Then sheep were put out to graze and the rabbits moved in. Together, they effectively destroyed the natural vegetation cover and let loose enormous sand drifts which rolled on the township and eventually engulfed it.

Introduced plants have also become noxious pests. The decorative lantana, native of the Americas, runs riot in our tropical and subtropical coastal areas. Round the ghost town of Ravenswood in north Queensland a blue-flowering shrub called Rubber Vine has taken over the whole countryside. Most spectacular among plant pests is Paterson's Curse. An Albury man, Paterson, brought it in for his garden in 1869. It did very nicely. Now thousands of square kilometres of country from New South Wales across to South Australia suffocate under the brilliant purple blooms. The sight is spectacular, but so is the damage to pastures.

Place names on the map tell the story of colonial optimism and hardships: on one hand Hope Valley, Kind Valley, Paradise; and Wilson's Downfall, Mount Disappointment, The Risk, Wail and Broke on the other. But whatever the difficulties, there can be no doubt that in the final analysis the land has proved immensely productive.

Of the total landmass, sixty-five per cent is now used for farming in one form or another. An overwhelming ninety-six per cent of this area is only suitable for grazing livestock, the rainfall being too low for crops to survive. Not only is Australia the world's flattest landmass, but it is the driest too. Properties abutting the central desert need to be vast if they are to be at all economical. In the outlying districts on the verges of the desert, graziers can at best stock 10 000 sheep on 200 000 acres (80 900 hectares). It is a measure of the

1 *University students on vacation sort prawns aboard a trawler.*

2 *Commercial fishermen cleaning their barramundi catch. Barramundi, or giant perch, is prized throughout the country for its sweet, succulent flesh. The hefty silver-grey fish which can weigh up to 50 kilograms are caught in Australia's tropical waters.*

3 *Some would call this fair retribution: a turnabout where man eats shark. Incidents where shark eats man are out of all proportion to the fear they evoke. There are, in fact, only some 50 attacks worldwide each year and only half that number are fatal. Of that total very few occur in Australian waters. Here at Ulladulla, New South Wales, shark is offloaded for later sale as the ubiquitous 'flake and chips' — a popular item on the Australian menu.*

Following page 1 *The Maryvale Mill at Morwell, Victoria, belongs to Australian Paper Manufacturers (APM). Australia produces over 70 per cent of her total paper and paperboard requirements.*

2 *Near Taree, New South Wales, a timbercutter brings down a mighty hardwood.*

3 *Dead tree landscape exposed by drought at Lake Cawndilla, New South Wales.*

1

2

3

1

sparseness of vegetation that each sheep needs twenty acres (eight hectares) to survive. Nevertheless, this dry rural land is cheap in Australia and in money terms the yield can be high. In the case of sheep, the 140 million in the country produce about a third of the world's wool. Mutton and lamb are valuable exports, too, and the strange sight of thousands of sheep being herded aboard converted oil tankers makes the point. They are shipped live to supply Middle Eastern orders which specify the animals must be slaughtered according to the strict rules of Islam.

Beef cattle cope better in a hot climate without extreme variations, so they are raised widely in the north and across most parts of Australia except the central western desert. Approximately half the total beef production is exported, much of it to Europe and Japan.

Despite the rigours of drought — in the early 1980s as fierce as any on record — the wheat industry remains dominant. In 1982-83 it had once again risen to be the single largest earner of foreign currency.

The country offers such an enormous range of climatic conditions that an astonishing array of crops thrives, from sugarcane and

1 *A blast at Mt Newman loosens iron ore for the huge mechanical shovels to remove.*

2 *Lang Hancock, a man whose potential wealth is as incalculable as the iron ore deposits he owns, with his daughter and heir, Gina. Just over 30 years ago, Hancock discovered quite by chance the huge iron ore deposits of the Pilbara, Western Australia. He revealed his find to Rio Tinto Mining Co. of Australia and is paid a royalty on every tonne of ore mined.*

3 *A construction worker, South Australia.*

4 *Ingots in the making at Whyalla, South Australia.*

2

3

4

cotton to snow peas and raspberries. The two great problems, shortage of water and the poor quality of much of the soil, have been countered to some extent by irrigation and by the heavy use of superphosphate. Because insects proliferate, often in plague proportions, insecticides have also become an essential factor in food production.

Not all revenue comes from products that originated overseas. Profits are still made from hunting native animals, particularly muttonbirds and kangaroos. Each year on the Bass Strait islands, hundreds of thousands of muttonbirds are caught in their burrows before they are fully fledged, cooked in vats and exported as a delicacy to Asia. Although there is considerable public outcry, the government permits the slaughter of kangaroos for pet food and for their skins. More than three million a year are commercially killed, the largest share of this 'harvest' being one and a half million in Queensland. The Ministry for Home Affairs and the Environment argues that farmers are concerned that their crops will be damaged by too many kangaroos and in these circumstances it is necessary to safeguard their livelihood. Notably, Victoria does not permit the killing of kangaroos though it processes those shot in other states.

Another natural resource constantly 'harvested' is timber. The industry depends heavily on native forests which, as a result of clear-felling, have dwindled swiftly. Three-quarters of all logs are cut from these areas. But forestry planners expect this proportion will drop to half by the end of the century when many of the planted conifer forests come to maturity. The native timbers — slow-growing hardwoods, many with clean straight grain — are milled for building materials and paper manufacture. In recent years, the state forestry departments have clashed with conservationists on the export of woodchips to Japan and the logging of rainforests which often do not regenerate, or do so at a very slow rate.

1 *Giant among the giants, Broken Hill Proprietary Co. Ltd (more commonly called BHP) controls most of the mining, refining and manufacturing of iron and steel in this country. The Newcastle Steelworks, ablaze with light as it works round the clock, is but one of several such fabrication plants. After 1955, Japan's burgeoning steel industry provided the main export market for Australian iron ore, but the worldwide recession of the 1980s and competitive prices from countries such as Brazil and South Africa have taken a large bite from the market. This downturn left a scar on the industry. But, a positive effect has been new initiatives for fresh markets. Australia ranks as the third greatest producer of iron ore after the Soviet Union and Brazil.*

2 *There is more to the Australian boat-building industry than winged keels and yachts. This large rig tender decked with scaffolding is under construction at Cockburn Sound, Western Australia.*

1

2

3

4

The cultivation, since the Second World War, of radiata pine forests to supply the demand for softwoods should do much to protect the indigenous timbers. But even this forward planning is unlikely to change the fact that more timber and timber products are imported into the country than are exported.

Japan is often in the Australian news, usually in terms of some multi-million dollar deal between the two countries. When it comes to fishing, however, Japan and Taiwan are accused of poaching in Australian territorial waters. Australia claims a zone of 200 nautical miles of surrounding sea, which provides rich grounds for fishing fleets operating in all states. The boats are mainly privately owned and run, with the catch being marketed through co-operatives. Foreign encroachment is a bitter issue.

Whale oil was one of the earliest exports and whaling stations once dotted the coast from Queensland to Tasmania and Western Australia. Whales are now protected in Australian waters and the stations have been dismantled, abandoned or put to other use.

From the point of view of overseas income, no other sector has shown such amazing growth as the mining industry. Within a mere thirty years the whole economy has been transformed by the discovery of mineral wealth beyond imagining. It has seen an economic upheaval every bit as great as the discovery of gold a century earlier. Though the greatest money is still in coal and iron, which were already being mined a hundred years ago, we now make profits from minerals — such as bauxite — scarcely heard of then.

Australia has a history of mining going back to the discovery of coal in 1791, but these early finds prepared no one for the extravaganza of riches the country is yielding today. Open-cut mines scoop out whole tracts of land for brown coal in Victoria and black in New South Wales. Using a new process, the Japanese have set up a pilot plant on one of Victoria's coalfields to produce oil from coal. The bauxite mines of north Queensland are the largest in the world, while in the Pilbara district of Western Australia and at Iron Monarch in South Australia colossal machines gouge away mountains of iron ore.

Only in a land so sparsely populated could mining on this scale make so little impression on living space and leave the general community so untouched in all respects but export income. This indifference has begun to be challenged by the still young but virile conservation movement which is making the public increasingly aware of what lies ahead, the larger implications of land abuse and the need for public concern and action.

The most direct effect has been felt by Aborigines moved off their tribal grounds. They have had to come to terms with the bitter reality that areas acknowledged as theirs can be taken away if the state governments find a lucrative use for them. The law courts have tussled with the issue of Aboriginal land rights and the royalties to be paid to people whose rights lie not in sheafs of deeds and papers but in a tradition of residence that goes back thousands of years.

Uranium is the most contentious of all the country's resources. The argument against mining is based on two factors: the worldwide risks resulting from nuclear power capacity inevitably leading to nuclear weapons capacity; and the fact that the waste can never be disposed of, though modern techniques may render it inert. Australia, having a fifth of the entire world supply, is in a strong position to influence international policy by refusing to exploit

Previous page: Huge bucket excavators dwarfed by the size of coal stockpiles at Hay Pt, Queensland. The bucket excavator is gradually replacing the underground miner as more and more open-cut mines are developed. Australia's truly staggering coal reserves are of varying quality — from brown coal to anthracite — and by world standards they are both readily accessible and contain thick coal seams. Not only do coal exports earn valuable foreign exchange now, but with the expected rise in liquid fuel prices, oil-from-coal projects will become a viable proposition.

2 A straight red gash marks the path of the Moonie/Jackson natural gas pipeline.

3 Loading iron ore at Mt Newman, the largest iron ore mine in Australia.

4 One of Australia's five-million-strong workforce.

1

2

3

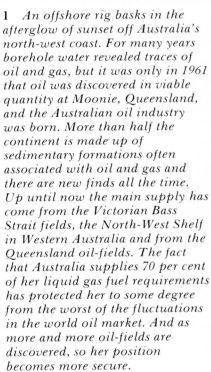

1 *An offshore rig basks in the afterglow of sunset off Australia's north-west coast. For many years borehole water revealed traces of oil and gas, but it was only in 1961 that oil was discovered in viable quantity at Moonie, Queensland, and the Australian oil industry was born. More than half the continent is made up of sedimentary formations often associated with oil and gas and there are new finds all the time. Up until now the main supply has come from the Victorian Bass Strait fields, the North-West Shelf in Western Australia and from the Queensland oil-fields. The fact that Australia supplies 70 per cent of her liquid gas fuel requirements has protected her to some degree from the worst of the fluctuations in the world oil market. And as more and more oil-fields are discovered, so her position becomes more secure.*

2 *Fuel storage tanks in evening light.*

3 *Instructions on the job.*

these deposits. The counter argument is that a fifth is only a fifth and if Australia does not mine and sell her uranium (not to mention the other valuable minerals that are the by-products), others will step up production and supply the market. The question is asked: with the country still reeling from recession, can the government turn its back on a source of revenue so badly needed? For the present, mining has been resumed.

The remaining power fuels are natural gas, huge supplies of which are found — notably on the north-west shelf — and petroleum. The oil, most of it piped from Bass Strait rigs, fills some seventy per cent of national needs. To maintain that percentage a great deal more has to be tapped. The mineral exploration companies are in a strong position because, although they now have to drill deeper and to more inaccessible levels than ever before and bear the cost of this, some of the guesswork has gone out of searching. No longer are discoveries being made by geologists simply following hunches and testing samples. Even aerial survey is inadequate. The Landsat satellite bounces infra-red rays off the earth, obtaining a profile not available through any other means. Sophisticated computing and micro-processing equipment interpret the data collected and huge mining corporations, such as MIM, BHP, CSR, CRA and Western Mining, gain valuable information that guides them in their search.

Now that the extent of Australia's saleable treasures is becoming known the questions move from the merely practical to the political: matters such as foreign ownership of our resources, emphasis on export rather than on the refining and processing of minerals for an Australian manufacturing sector and, above all, the consequences of mining with concern only for the present and not the future.

1   *Transporting iron ore, Mt Newman. The lid of Australia's mineral treasure-house has hardly been prised open, yet already it reveals astounding riches in coal, bauxite, mineral sands, copper, nickel, manganese and uranium. The discovery of diamond-bearing volcanic pipes in Western Australia has added yet another gem to the nation's wealth. All this has thrust the country into world prominence as a source of raw materials. Today 21 per cent of all exports are mineral-based and, of this, 42 per cent is destined for Japan.*

2   *At work on the Jackson/Moonie pipeline.*

2

3

4

3 *Bright yellow uranium-bearing ore piled up at the Ranger mine, Northern Territory. Immense deposits at places such as Jabiluka, Yeelirrie, Ranger and at South Australia's controversial Roxby Downs, give Australia a fifth of the world's known reserves. Few issues have proved as divisive in the 1980s as the mining of uranium. Although the Hawke government has decided to permit the mining and export of uranium to continue, there are powerful lobbies working to close the mines and stop Australia taking part in the nuclear industry with its potential dangers to mankind.*

4 *In the outback the motor car is a vital means of keeping in touch with the outside world; in the cities it is often a symbol of material success and an outlet for aggression. Not surprisingly, recession hit the industry hard. Factories were closed and people laid off from a labour force that numbered 70 000 in 1981. But as things look up, as optimism returns, Australians once more eye the motor showrooms and dream of the open road. Here Fords come off the production line at the Melbourne plant.*

Beyond the Pale: State Boundaries

This, then, is the cake. How it has been divided up is another matter — for the most part, a combination of accident and opportunism. For a start, the state boundaries have little to do with this marvellous and various country. In only two places do the boundaries and the landscape match: along the Murray River that divides New South Wales from Victoria, and where the upper reaches of the Macintyre lead to a pass in the McPherson Range between New South Wales and Queensland. The rest is purely a matter of right angles and ruled lines.

As soon as a colony was granted self-government, it set about consolidating its own interests. Each saw its principal rivals as the others. From the start, scrupulous attention was given to keeping wealth from seeping across the border. Indeed, ever since it was formed in 1901, the Federation has remained an uneasy one. Cheerful insults about banana-benders and crow-eaters are still traded across the imaginary lines drawn between one loyalty and another.

The legacy of division and dislocated services is apparent in many aspects of Australian life. To me there's no more telling a symbol of inter-state relations than the railways. Railways not only revolutionised land transport in the nineteenth century but threatened to breach state insularity. Local legislators regarded train travel as potentially disastrous and so, to prevent each other getting in, and to prevent their own produce getting out through any but the state's own ports, they built incompatible rail systems.

New South Wales chose the standard English gauge of 4 feet 8½ inches (143.5 cm), so the neighbouring states made sure they didn't. Victoria, went one grander with 5 feet 3 inches (160 cm), while Queensland decided on a modest 3 feet 6 inches (106.5 cm). Western Australia, having no common boundary with Queensland, could safely put in 3 feet 6 inches; so could Tasmania, being adequately insulated from all the rest by Bass Strait. South Australia, apparently willing to please everybody, had lines of all three gauges. Superimposed on this state-run grid, Commonwealth Railways built a second system to overcome the century-old

Seen from above, the bold and soaring exterior shells of the Sydney Opera House reveal the brilliance of Danish architect Joern Utzon whose design was selected in 1957 from more than 230 entries in a world-wide competition. Controversial when building began, today the Opera House is acknowledged as one of the architectural landmarks of the twentieth century and is listed by the World Heritage Council. Since its official opening in October 1973, millions of Australians and visitors have enjoyed the splendid productions staged in the various performing halls. At night, galaxies of splintered light play on the water, and the Opera House seems to sail free on Sydney Harbour.

suspicions; using one gauge they linked all capitals except Darwin. Yet even as recently as the 1950s, goods travelling by rail from Perth to Brisbane had to be transhipped five times on the way.

One great enterprise of co-operation was in the building of the famous dingo-proof fence to protect sheep. Entered in the *Guinness Book of Records* as the longest fence in the world, it involved agreements between three state governments (Queensland, New South Wales and South Australia) and stretched for some 5531 kilometres. Revenue for upkeep was raised from property owners by means of a wild-dog tax. Now a large percentage of Queensland properties have switched from sheep to beef cattle, the dingoes are no longer a threat to them, so the government decided in 1982 to discontinue full maintenance on the fence. No doubt some state loyalist took satisfaction in washing hands of this collaboration.

During my adolescence in Brisbane I frequented (among other delights of that eccentric city) the old museum. One particular exhibit gave me more pleasure and amusement than the others: a pair of showcases side by side. In design they were identical, huge Victorian affairs with stained cedar frames and large panes of imperfect plate glass. One carried the gold-leaf legend *Queensland Marsupials* and contained a stuffed wallaby or two, a kangaroo, a couple of possums, an echidna and a koala bear. The other, labelled *Southern Marsupials*, contained a stuffed wallaby or two, a kangaroo, a couple of possums, an echidna and a koala bear; the difference was that these unfortunates had been found on the nether side of the border.

To us Queenslanders it was a bit of a joke. But underneath, I have to admit, we had quite different feelings for those two displays. We looked on our marsupials as rather endearing because they were ours. The others, being foreigners, aroused benign but dispassionate curiosity. Possibly we viewed people from 'The South', as we called

1 *Tempting Lady Luck on her wedding night, a bride plays the 'pokies' (poker machines) at a club in Broken Hill, New South Wales. The League clubs, their reputations unhappily tarnished recently with allegations of organised crime in New South Wales, offer a place to get together to relax with mates and enjoy often lavish entertainments.*

2 *One of the world's most mellow and orderly subtropical cities, Brisbane is relaxed and lovely. While the city centre on the banks of the Brisbane River shares much with cities elsewhere in Australia, the suburbs are distinctive: the houses with broad verandahs ideal for good neighbourliness on balmy evenings are perched on stilts to catch cool breezes.*

3 *An hour's drive south of Brisbane lies the Gold Coast with its special style. The elderly come here to have old bones warmed by the gentle sun; the young come to live out fantasies summed up by the litany of sun, fun and surf — and the chance of becoming a Playboy centrefold.*

2

3

1, 3 *Stepping out at Inflation disco, Melbourne. Australia's nightlife is as varied as human fantasy will allow — from an evening of gentle slumming to wild raves for the uninhibited (3).*

2 *One of the highlights of the gay community's social calendar — the Alternative Miss World Contest. Glamour and fantasy are the keynotes of this fancy dress ball which culminates in the crowning of the 'Alternative Miss World'.*

1

everywhere else except the Northern Territory, in much the same way. This was all very comforting and proved in some unarguable sense that we were best. If anyone had told us that people in Cairns regarded us as 'Southerners' too, we would have clobbered the liar. On second thoughts, nothing so deeply destructive to the meaning of life was conceivable to us so we would probably have called him a crow-eater and let him off with a warning.

In terms of international comparisons, Brisbane is remarkable — it must be the only city of a million people in a subtropical climate that is hygienic, without slums, free from epidemic disease, and all parts of which are completely open and free to all citizens. The summers are muggy and at 5.07 each evening thunder bangs away; the rain is so heavy it spurts back off the road white as fur. Then the storm is gone. Thick foliage throughout the suburbs drips greenly and steam rises from hot roads that switchback round the hilly suburbs. To cool down, neighbours sit out on their broad, sagging verandahs. Many houses are set high off the ground on piles. Under the house, the men, a glass of beer ever in reach, tinker with the car. They hitch up their shorts, swat a couple of mosquitoes and shake their heads at what a stinker it will be tomorrow.

But to find real expertise in the weather, there is nowhere to match Perth. Perth people are tremendously proud of their weather. Unlike the east coast cities which have hot wet summers and cool dry winters, Perth has its rain in winter and a summer that lasts for eight months of brilliant, predictable sunshine. And if Queenslanders think 'The South' is remote and antagonistic to their interests, how much more remote is 'The East' from Perth. Not only does this encourage them to criticise the rest, but the Western Australians have turned the distance into a virtue as well — by making sure they can provide anything they want for themselves.

This casual, colourful city of 902 000 is exceptionally well equipped with recreation grounds, waterways and parks. A bus driver explained to me: 'We'll hang in with the rest of Australia while it suits us. But now we've got the money, with the minerals and that, we can go it alone any time we like.'

This is not a new attitude. Western Australia was the last state to agree to federation. What is more, in 1933 it voted to secede. It is only

Previous page: *Dawn announces the most famous skyline of them all — Sydney Harbour.*

1 *Dining alfresco in the Rocks area of Sydney.*

2 *Pier One was the disembarkation point for immigrants in the past, but for today's visitors it is a charmingly remodelled part of the city, filled with cafes, shops and a tavern in nostalgic style.*

3 *When the Sydney Harbour Bridge was built in 1932, the foresight of the city fathers was astonishing: it was designed to carry up to 6000 vehicles an hour as well as provide for trains and pedestrians at a time when the North Shore was barely populated. Their aim of linking the North Shore with the metropolitan area and thus encouraging Sydneysiders to live across the water was more effective than they could ever have dreamt. As this evening traffic shows, the trip home over the bridge has become a motorist's nightmare and a second bridge must surely be built. However, in the affections of the citizens and as a symbol of the city, nothing can replace it.*

4 *An entertainer at Pier One.*

5 *Roselands Shopping Centre, expresses all the razzle-dazzle and unabashed commercialism that give Sydney its special vitality.*

2

3

4

5

1

2

3

4

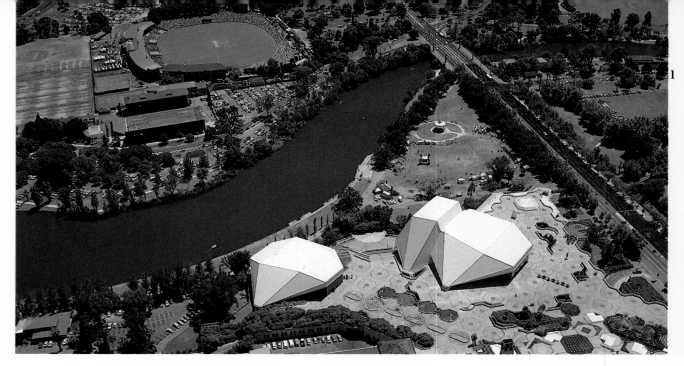

thanks to King George V that it is still part of the Commonwealth of Australia — his government refused to ratify the secession.

Perth has enjoyed a fresh upsurge of local pride with the winning of the America's Cup by the Western Australian yacht *Australia II*. Having beaten the best America could offer, no wonder they feel on top of the world.

Despite the immensity of the continent as a whole, most Australian cities suffer the universal problems of not knowing how to accommodate a population far too large for their resources and how to cope with far too many cars converging onto the central area. Thirty years ago the answers seemed clear: low-cost multi-storey accommodation and a complex system of motorways. So, down came a lot of houses to make room for the new estates and down came a lot more houses to clear a path for the big roads. The only capitals to escape the worst horrors of these mistakes were Adelaide and Hobart.

Adelaide, from the beginning, was a privileged city. The residents congratulated themselves on never having had convicts and the fact that Colonel Light bequeathed them a plan of broad streets and ample parklands round which well-placed suburbs have grown. The city also boasts handsome buildings of pink hued freestone and an Arts Festival that is nationally renowned. As it turns out, Adelaide's greatest privilege, in the opinion of many, is being so handy to the wine-growing districts of McLaren Vale and the Barossa Valley.

The Barossa is a mere half hour's drive away, up from the rectilinear streets of the city, through gullies and gorges. Most of the wineries are open daily for tastings and sales, and many Adelaide people, as well as visitors to the state, submit themselves to temptation, sampling the vintners' extensive range of reds and whites.

Hobart, on the other hand, certainly had convicts and developed round its port in an organic, thoroughly quirky and visually delightful way. The reason Hobart has been saved the worst of twentieth-century urban disfigurement is lack of the huge population growth of the other capitals. With only 170 200 people, it is one-sixth the size of Brisbane and one-twentieth of Sydney.

Previous page **1** *Melbourne's version of the Eiffel Tower; a steel and aluminium structure that soars above the Victorian Arts Centre. Plans for the centre were put forward over 20 years ago but the Concert Hall was only opened in 1982.*

2 *'A flower for a flower,' were the words of housewife Mila Markovina as she handed a pink carnation to Diana, Princess of Wales as she and Prince Charles left the Melbourne Concert Hall after a gala performance in their honour. Despite growing republican rumblings, the ecstatic reception given to the royal couple on their 1983 tour left no doubt that many Australians still feel great loyalty to the Royal Family.*

3 *The Little River Band in concert.*

4 *Melbourne's somewhat staid city streets are slowly being transformed. This filigree of steel and glass covers the Great Space at Collins Place in the city.*

1 South Australian number plates carry the legend 'Festival State' — a reference to the now-famous Arts Festival that takes place in Adelaide biennially. The main site of this marvellous feast of culture is the Festival Centre on the banks of the Torrens River.

2 Poetry readings and the music of such luminaries as Yehudi Menuhin, Vladimir Ashkenazy and the London Philharmonic Orchestra are just a few of the attractions of the Festival. Ballet, opera and exhibitions of paintings and sculpture are also featured in this setting which is in itself a work of art.

3 Stainless steel balls by sculptor Burt Flugelman in Adelaide's delightful Rundle Mall.

4 Australia's insularity in the past has had a dual effect on her public art collections and museums. On one hand they reflect the need to support and encourage the artists working in this country and breaking new ground; on the other there is the powerful argument that we should also be acquiring works by international masters to enrich the local cultural experience. This majestic mother figure by Henry Moore is at the National Gallery of Victoria.

The whole island of Tasmania evokes colonial echoes almost lost elsewhere, not just in its English-style fields and old stone farmhouses, but in the numerous convict-built bridges and gaols. The Port Arthur ruins are the most extensive of all Australia's surviving convict buildings. In their beautiful setting, the roofless cells, church and barracks still call up the ghosts of human suffering too dreadful to believe any civilised race could inflict on its people. But these disturbing reminders of the real world are gradually being dispelled by tourists, who arrive in ever-increasing swarms.

Isolation has been a moulding force. Tasmanian individuality is largely a product of being cut off. As 'The South' is to Queenslanders and 'The East' to Western Australians, so 'The Mainland' is to Tasmanians. Left behind in the minerals boom, Hobart has become a conservative town, a trifle prim, with a Sunday feeling some claim lasts throughout the week. Perhaps, for this very reason, they built Australia's first casino there. Quietly and sensibly, Hobart has adjusted, as an elderly person might to a wart on one cheek.

The casino is all red plush and glitter inside, while outside yachts ride at anchor in the harbour. A fine powdering of rain sweeps by on the wind, and Mount Wellington rises close behind the city, yet seeming remote as a strange planet looming over the horizon. Beyond the roulette wheels and the traditional Australian two-up game, far higher stakes are being gambled for as the hydro-electric authority claims more and more of the island for dams and water catchment in the name of economic survival.

Only once in living memory has Tasmania presented the nation with an issue big enough to affect the outcome of a Federal election. This was the decision to flood the last great wilderness area in the south-west, the Gordon-Franklin River system. It also changed the image of conservation from an issue of interest only to the 'Greenies' and a minority on the fringe, to a matter of concern to the mainstream. The NO DAMS campaign had the entire population by the ears. And even after Bob Hawke's Labor government came to power with its promise to stop the dam, the Tasmanian government took the case to the High Court. It became the most sustained moral cliff-hanger since the withdrawal of Australian troops from the Vietnam War in 1972.

Previous page: Perth is still revelling in its new-found status of yachting capital of the world. The spirit of sail and city is perfectly expressed by these yachts heeling on the Swan River.

1 *As an elderly couple scans the names inscribed upon the Roll of Honour in Canberra's War Memorial, youngsters stroll by oblivious. To the generations born after the two World Wars, they are just names, but to older Australians they are a powerful memory and unifying force.*

2 *With Melbourne and Sydney vying for the role of national capital, the decision to create a city specifically for the purpose of government appeared a rational solution. And so Canberra and the Australian Capital Territory were born. There are many who believe that decisions made by people away from the real commercial and population centres of the country do not always reflect the national mood. But while they may accuse the city of public service blandness, they cannot but admire its well laid out streets, cared-for gardens and handsome public buildings such as the High Court seen here.*

2

3   Set on Black Mountain and
backed by the undulating
landscape that surrounds the city,
one of Canberra's landmarks, the
Telecommunication Tower.

4   After lunch, delegates make
their way back to the Houses of
Parliament for the 1983 Economic
Summit. Symbol of Bob Hawke's
'government by consensus', the
summit in retrospect had more
impact in terms of public relations
than as a tool of policy-making.

3

4

The wilderness is still there and, as a bonus to Tasmania, is now the third most famous natural feature of the country, after Ayers Rock and the Great Barrier Reef. The long term effect on revenue is likely to be healthy for the state and may gentle resentment of workers who felt the rug pulled from under their feet. Tasmania suffered the bite of economic recession no less than the rest of the country. The value of wilderness to mankind in the future versus a pay packet today was a clear-cut choice for many Tasmanians.

The first pioneer families to move into Victoria arrived there by ship from Van Diemen's Land, as Tasmania was then called. They were men of property and tradesmen looking for room to expand, free from the restrictions of the redcoat military government. When Melbourne was established as the port for this area, a special relationship was born — one which still exists. The inland cities of Ballarat and (especially) Bendigo have the character of extensions of Melbourne in its more flamboyant mood. No other Australian capital has quite this closeness to its provinces, nor quite this solid backing. And yet Melbournians tend to look on their city as gypsies might an aged relative who has settled down in a sober stone house to a routine slightly shameful in its respectability. Energetically as they may declare its superiority to Sydney, I suspect (as an outsider to both cities) that beneath that stiff upper lip they harbour a secret longing to kick over the traces, to live the loose blowsy life of the rival.

People here have an air of preoccupation about them, each appearing to be a person of consequence, right in the middle of conducting some unhurried business. This tolerant, comfortable city has Australia's best public transport, the best and most varied restaurants, a pub on just about every corner, and by far the finest art gallery. And something lurks beneath the surface, something Sydneysiders do not have. Crowds intermingle like members of a club. The focal point of Sydney is its harbour; Melbourne's focal point is its people. The 'club' is united, I think, by two things. Firstly, Australian Rules football and, secondly, a legacy from the city's history, from the optimism of the mid-nineteenth century when it was founded, a kind of faith in the common good. This is not active, has little political or even civic expression. But it keeps

1 *Where the other towns and cities have their horse races, Alice Springs puts on its annual Camel Cup. Camels were introduced to Australia from 1840 onwards and have done sterling service in the arid regions of the continent. Explorers, telegraph line builders and a host of others made use of these ill-tempered beasts. Thousands roam free in the Australian outback.*

2 *The Top End in the 'wet' — the four months of summer when tropical rain lashes the region and cyclones can cause devastation.*

2

3

4

3   *Darwin as it is today, rebuilt after Cyclone Tracy in 1974 ravaged the city, leaving rubble and shattered lives in its wake. Philosophically, the citizens tidied the wreckage and started all over again — with a little more attention to building structures able to withstand natural disasters. With almost 62 000 people, Darwin is the fastest growing Australian city.*

4   *Fishermen at Darwin Harbour perch some ten metres above the water at low tide, revealing the tremendous tidal fluctuations in the Timor Sea.*

people from losing heart, gives them an everyday reliability, as though someone has said, if we stick together we'll be all right.

As for football, the great Melbourne names are not remote television personalities, but men you can go and watch in the flesh any Saturday of the Aussie Rules season. The names themselves tell another story too: Duperouzel, Bosustow, Van der Haar, Daicos, Foschini, Buhagiar and Schimmelbusch. Though many people find them exotic, you never hear anyone get them wrong and the men themselves are as Australian in manner, accent and attitude as pie and sauce or pizza or sweet and sour pork . . . so powerful is the pull of this rough and aerial game that just about everyone is drawn into debating details of play in last Saturday's match.

Sydney is quite the opposite. There is little sense of network with the provincial cities of New South Wales. Indeed, it firmly faces the Pacific, rejoicing in the beaches and the harbour. Sydney without its harbour would be unthinkable. This is one of the world's great sites. To a visitor travelling on a Hunters Hill ferry, let's say, dazzled by sunshine, hair raked back by the wind, head filled with a smell of the open sea, it is hard to believe this is how many people go to work each day. The light, the air, the dramatic gesture of the Harbour Bridge and the Opera House are so persuasively glamorous that the most routine journey smacks of a holiday.

What use is it to say the majority lives twenty kilometres away in the redbrick suburbs, or that pollution levels are sometimes so high a sandy-coloured cloud broods over the city, or that derelicts are a common sight fishing in rubbish bins for survival? The spirit of the place is so vital, so braggart, it seems churlish to resist. And on weekends, the sixty kilometres of suburban beaches are crammed with sun-lovers: not just those who live in the lucky parts of the city. Everybody goes to the beach and the pleasure costs no more than the train or bus fare to get there.

1 *Architecturally reminiscent of the grand old cotton plantations of the American 'Deep South', Clarendon House at Nile, Tasmania, is one of many gracious and romantic dwellings that attract tourists.*

2 *Ironically, Australia's first casino, Wrest Point, was built in Tasmania — the state invariably portrayed as conservative and quiet. 'Mainlanders' — particularly people from Victoria where casinos have yet to be legalised — bolster the Tasmanian tourist figures.*

2

3 4

3 *Sympathetically restored merchant warehouses line Salamanca Place in Hobart.*

4 *The ravages of Queenstown's mining history are evident on these barren slopes that were once covered with lush rain-forest. The discovery of gold and copper here in 1883 attracted miners and a settlement grew up that, by the turn of the century, ranked third in size after Hobart and Launceston.*

Australia has no frontiers other than the sun and the sea. Travelling outback towards the desert, the sun eventually becomes a barrier to survival itself. In the other direction, the traveller is stopped by the sea. In this sense Sydney looks out as a frontier town with all the razzle-dazzle of advertising a good time and no questions asked.

Only Darwin has this frontier mentality more markedly. Even so, the people there are very much aware of being in the Northern Territory and that prosperity depends on the Territory's rich mineral resources, the beef industry and the tourists passing through town on their way to Ayers Rock.

At the other end of the scale is Canberra's country town *chic,* so cool and dry, its architecture like that of the new European satellite cities, its cared-for streets on which its cared-for citizens may occasionally be seen.

Each year in January, musicians from all over the country converge on Canberra for the Australian Summer School of Early Music. The campus resounds to the famous voice of Gerald English

1 *Carved by relentless seas, the Twelve Apostles dominate the soaring coastline in Victoria's Port Campbell National Park.*
Of Australia's 36 735 kilometres of coastline, this stretch is considered by many to be the most imposing.

1

2

2   To the early settlers the Blue Mountains 75 kilometres inland of Sydney seemed an insurmountable barrier; to Sydneysiders today they are a welcome retreat of primeval loveliness.

3   Although women have made great progress in breaking down Australia's traditionally male-dominated society, fishing weekends 'with the boys' are still part of the way of life for many. This campsite on the Murray epitomises this ethic: men, boat, beer and the great outdoors.

3

rehearsing Rameau. The exquisite harmonies of Louis XIV's palace at Versailles go drifting out to the nation's capital, trembling in the dry summer air, to be faintly heard at the earthworks where a new parliament house has begun to rise from the ruins of a hill.

Canberra has been described as less a city than a giant garden with buildings sprinkled among the trees. Even so, it is no Versailles. The courtiers at Versailles were convinced theirs was the centre of the civilised world. Canberra is predominantly a public service town, but the public servants tend to be apologetic about what they do, which comes from being treated disrespectfully by the rest of the country. Australians make a national virtue of treating authority with suspicion. Briefly, when Gough Whitlam was in power (1972-75), Canberra flickered to life as the true centre of power and exciting decisions. Perhaps it will come again. Until such time, the people make do with comfort, clean air and fine facilities.

If Canberra is accused of being bland — well, blandness is the consequence of going along with the mainstream. This is the kind of life the majority of people elsewhere are struggling to achieve, the routine satisfactions we're constantly being warned about by those who move against the current, against self-satisfaction as an ambition, against computer technology as a religion, and against money as the ultimate happiness.

1 *You could be forgiven for thinking that in Australia used-boat dealers outnumber those selling second-hand cars. A new trend is 'bare boat chartering' where craft such as this, the classically proportioned 'Capricorn Dancer' sailing in the Whitsunday Passage off the Queensland coast, are available for hire. You provide supplies and crew.*

2 *The sunny faces of teenagers on a Queensland beach.*

3 *Holidaymakers are swirled through the sea on a net dragged by a boat. 'Boom-netting', as it is called, is tremendously popular on the Queensland coast.*

2   3

2

1   Surfers Paradise on the Gold
Coast — the most developed,
colourful, commercialised and
publicised holiday area in
Australia. Taking advantage of the
natural attributes of fine weather
and magnificent surf beaches,
property developers have outdone
one another here to make every
centimetre a paying proposition.
Their handiwork creates an all but
continuous backdrop of highrise
buildings.

2   Standard beach attire — a tan
and little else.

3 Most Australians live on or near the coast and seem obsessed with sea and sun. Here crowds pack Half Moon Bay near Melbourne.

4 The ancient Egyptians might well have felt an affinity with us: here a sun-worshipper is anointed with oil.

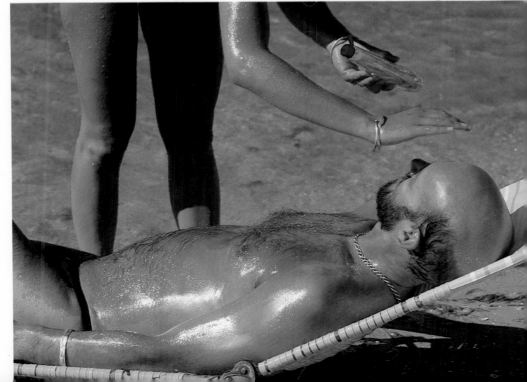

1   *A terrestrial paradise in the azure setting of the Great Barrier Reef.*

2   *The underwater splendour of the Great Barrier Reef tends to distract prospective visitors from the many other natural attributes along the coast. The birdlife, for example, is prolific and varied. Here lesser crested terns mingle with a few sooty terns while two common noddys look on.*

3   From the air, coral patterns the limpid seas of the Great Barrier Reef. In 1981 the 1250 nautical mile-long Great Barrier Reef System was awarded the highest conservation status by the World Wildlife Heritage organisation, confirming the Reef's value not only to Australians but to the world.

4   Shimmering back from the surface, staghorn coral and just some of the jewel-like fish that inhabit the Reef.

1   *The national fascination with water is perhaps understandable on a continent where fresh water is so scarce. At play on the Murray River.*

2   *Each year, colourfully garbed against the sun, some 500 canoeists pit themselves against the elements in the Red Cross Murray River Canoe Marathon — at 400 kilometres the longest canoe race in the world.*

2

1

3

4

3   Crossing the Snowy River at its source in the Kosciusko National Park, New South Wales. Nearby is Mt Kosciusko, at 2228 metres the highest mountain in Australia. The entire area attracts nature lovers, both in summer and in winter when snow blankets the landscape.

4   Making the most of a sunny day on Lake Bonney, South Australia.

1

3

2

1, 3 *To foreigners, whose preconceived idea of Australia is one of desert, scenes such as this come as a surprise. In winter the area under snow along the south-eastern regions of the country is more extensive than the snowfields of Switzerland. Thousands flock to resorts to experience the thrill of skiing (3).*

2 *Climbers on the rock pinnacle of Little Horn Mountain, Tasmania. The mountain wilderness areas of Tasmania appeal to those who yearn to experience nature at its untamed best.*

Against the Current

BALD IS BEAUTIFUL. The car bearing this sticker on the rear bumper bar vanished in a hurricane of dust, heading out of Alice Springs, roughly speaking in the direction of Sri Lanka. Now if that isn't ostentatiously against the current among people increasingly obsessed by the fears and satisfactions of the mirror, I don't know what is.

For the most part, Australians are besotted with the average, the untalented, the low profile, the understatement and the underdog. Yet, curiously enough, eccentricity abounds. To foreign visitors we must appear full of anomalies. Among the most surprising is a fully operative Chinese josshouse right in the centre of Innisfail, a north Queensland sugar town. Although the story goes that until recently Italian could be heard spoken in the street as often as English, this is a solidly provincial place. Or is it? The Innisfail Opera Festival, held annually on the most stifling muggy days of December, gives warning that appearances may be misleading.

The members of the festival orchestra have another tale to tell. They travel thousands of kilometres for the fun of playing there. One year, after opening night, they plunged into the Johnstone River to escape the tormenting heat. As they revelled in the tepid water, pairs of red eyes were observed floating by: not exhausted fellow violinists, but the vigilant Johnstone River crocodiles.

The josshouse, painted red and gold with a brilliant green roof, is one of only three still in use for daily worship in Australia. When I was there, I found a young Chinese man standing outside. He smiled politely, perhaps a little nervously. 'I had to come to Australia to see one of these,' he explained. 'I am a student from Peking.'

In Innisfail or Melbourne or the back of Bourke, Australians are dazzled by modernity, innocently delighted by electronics, rushing headlong from one technological gewgaw to the next. Religious groups, preaching their unpalatable discomforts, have an uphill job. Salvation Army workers tend to look like aliens intent on the hopeless business of converting the pagans by good works.

I saw a posse of these worthy people recently at Manly Beach, Sydney, addressing a sprawl of surfers. The surfers, flaunting their Greek-god bodies, suntanned to within an inch of their lives, long bleached hair blowing, the sea waves calling, screwing up their eyes

Free-spirited mother and child at Byron Bay, New South Wales.

to chips of blue glass, nodded courteously. The Salvationists, buttoned in hot uniforms, wearing military hats and braid, clutching Bibles and tambourines, talked of heaven and the challenge to the conscience presented by the Permissive Society. But in that company, they were not the only ones defying materialism.

Many surfers themselves are part of a movement against the respectability of settling down to a career, raising a family and shackling the spirit with a house full of possessions. They claim to find a mystical relationship with the ocean. The waves become a force with cosmic implications. Surf magazines have developed a jargon of their own, vague, bombastic, evocative to their readers. Perhaps it is a sign of the times that recently they have begun undergoing a transition, publishing hardheaded articles on fitness, tactics and professionalism in competition. Even so, the surfers still wander the coasts, fanatical nomads who will do without anything but a board, a wetsuit and a seat in a vehicle. They draw the dole, take occasional casual work in winter, and present a notable uniformity of image. Yet their lifestyle stems from romantic notions of freedom, their passion for the sea has an innocence that is touched with something self-denying, something almost noble.

Another nature-worshipping minority which rejected mainstream values hit the news in 1973. The Aquarius Festival of the Australian Union of Students was held at Nimbin in northern New South Wales. This spectacular outdoor gathering, entertained by rock music, poetry readings and circus performers, drew thousands of devoted 'alternatives', students, middle class malcontents with mid-life crisis blues, hippies and hangers-on. Afterwards, hundreds stayed. Some invested in co-operatives like Tuntable Falls which sold 500 shares at $200 each to raise the $104 000 for the land. The prospectus explained: 'We seek land to set up an alternative community inhabited and designed by people concerned with surviving the century as one community. The community should see itself as an experimental one, dynamically developing the social structures and styles that a self-sufficient, ecologically balanced community might need.' The aim: 'to live in harmony with nature and ourselves, with love and understanding. To be free from pollution of air, food, bodies and mind.'

1   *In the restful setting of the Fremantle Arts Centre, Western Australia, a basket weaver at work. More and more people in towns and cities are learning crafts as a form of relaxation and self-expression as well as a means of making a living.*

2   *The first few precious moments as a father bonds with his newborn infant. Home births are highly controversial and the medical establishment has increasingly withdrawn its support for the practice.*

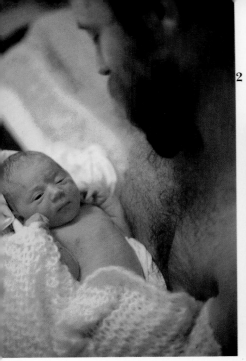

3　Seeking a different path from the mainstream, a young family at Great Keppel Island near the Great Barrier Reef.

4　A young potter at the wheel in Joan Campbell's renowned workshop in Fremantle, Western Australia. Like the rest of the western world, Australians face a future with a shorter working week and more leisure time to fill. Learning to use free time wisely and well is a growing experience and many have already turned to social work, study and creative pastimes in preparation.

3

4

Similar co-operatives have been set up by enthusiasts in other parts of the country. Their enemies among the small town conservatives claimed they were filthy, immoral and hotbeds of drug pushing and drug taking. In fact, most of them faced the real hardships of survival by basic farming and in their concern for cleanliness and physical good health they verged on the puritanical. Now, ten years later, these communities are firmly based round young families and represent the most substantial movement from the city back to the earth that the nation can show.

Far more widespread has been a seeking after craftsmanship. Perhaps to counteract the logic of mass-production, people increasingly try their hand at anything from mud-brick houses to pottery beads. Some observers, such as Barry Jones, Minister of Science and Technology, see this as more than a fringe group's hankering for a connection between what they use and what they make. He speaks of a future with its four-day working week — and the pleasures and perils of three days off to use as you will.

The crafts are booming. And the beauty of it is that people haven't simply developed a taste for the hand-made article as merchandise; they are out there weaving, carving, throwing and forging their own.

Even the financiers have had to take a fresh look at these movements. Alan Bond, millionaire chairman of the *Australia II* yacht syndicate, has bought the lease of the Nimbin Hotel in the heart of 'alternatives' territory. And, in keeping with the notion that in today's novel ideas lie the paths we may take tomorrow, BP Australia sponsored a remarkable solar car designed by Hans Tholstrup and Larry Perkins which, powered only by the sun, made the 4000-kilometre crossing of Australia.

At the opposite end of the transport scale and wholly incompatible with the surviving hippies and their vegetarian

1 *Bruce Arthur, one-time Olympic wrestler turned weaver, in his house on Dunk Island. In the great tradition of artist/eccentrics, Arthur has created a persuasively free lifestyle that attracts acolytes and the world-weary to his Barrier Reef retreat.*

2 *Saffron-robed members of the Hare Krishna movement out among the people whose values they reject. The spartan life on the ashrams is hard, almost puritan, with long hours of work and prayer.*

wholesomeness is another group rejecting social conformity — perhaps the most exclusive club in the land, the Hell's Angels. They have only a thousand members in the world, 150 of them in Australia. They are associated with Harley Davidson motorcycles, heavy rock music and violent brawls. This gives them a bad public image, but they don't care what people think. They live in a suburban fortress in Sydney behind high walls, with steel grilles on the windows and a remote-controlled front gate monitored by closed-circuit television. There is a sign saying 'STOP — do not pass this point. State your business here.' They say Hell's Angels is not just a social club, it is a lifestyle, and the public's fear is fear of the unknown. The public view, on the contrary, is that its fear is fear of the known — fear of violence.

The bikies, the alternatives, the surfies and the gays are all minorities who have made a conscious decision to reject at least some of the dominant social values. Others operate experimental schools to oppose the educational establishment. Some stand against the political mainstream and contest elections as the Marijuana Party, the Deadly Serious Party, or else join a faction of the Communist Party or the Right to Lifers. But perhaps the most conservative of those who set themselves against the current are the people resisting cultural values different to their own.

Various national associations put a great deal of effort into making sure they and their children do not forget the language, the music, the dance, the rituals and even the hereditary feuds of their homelands. For many, this is simply an occasional interest, centred round folklore and regional dress on feast days. For others it is a full-time attempt to resist cultural assimilation, while still regarding Australia as their home.

The Chassidic Jews began to arrive from Russia sixty years ago. This minority sect believes an intense participation in everyday living is also a means of serving God. Some Chassidic women cut their hair off when they marry and hide their heads under wigs for reasons of modesty. While, in the face of the narcissism of the cities around them, many of the men wear full beards and ear locks (side curls), long black coats and black hats.

Though the established Christian Churches have been in upheaval, chasing trends — their imitation Gothic arches shuddering to rock music, the traditionalists of their congregations shuddering at the English language mass and nuns in short skirts —fringe religions like the Hare Krishnas are going the opposite way. Thirsty for the rigours of monastic life, they pad in rumpled robes along the city streets. With shaven heads, a white daub on the forehead, they chant mantras to the indifferent shoppers.

Ironically, the Hare Krishna movement strongly echoes the values of puritan Christianity. The body is considered evil. The hair is cut off because it is a means of sexual attraction. Life in an ashram can be spartan. The faithful get up at 4 a.m. to begin chanting in the temple. After they have eaten, daily work is required of them. Not the least of their duties are those they perform out in the community from which they have cut themselves off, the community of their families, their schoolfellows, and the casual life in which so much may be taken for granted. Such commitment is not easy.

When considering the values of these various groups, the general public deserves acknowledgement: not only does it tolerate them, but has incorporated them to some extent.

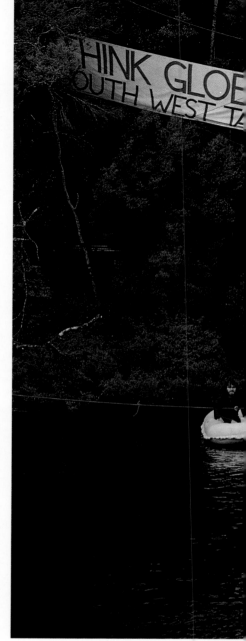

1 *Environmentalists have only just begun to win legitimacy in the eyes of the average Australian and the Tasmanian Wilderness issue has been the turning-point. When the Tasmanian government decided to dam the Gordon-below-Franklin river system, it also condemned forever an area of unsurpassed natural beauty and of immense botanical and archaeological interest. In a superbly orchestrated campaign led by Dr Bob Brown, the dam emerged as a matter not simply of interest to the 'Greenies' but to the public at large. In Tasmania itself, concerned people gathered to man blockades and make their*

1

objections felt. With an election looming, both political parties had to make their position clear. Once in office, the Hawke Government, honouring its election promise, stopped the building of the dam, thus giving environmentalists and future generations a major victory.

2   The anti-nuclear movement is extremely powerful, drawing support from all age groups and walks of life. An offshoot of this has been those who would like to see Australia dissociate itself from all forms of American militarism, including the American bases in this country.

2

In some cases, simply staying put is to take a stand against the mob. Survivors in a ghost town, for instance, have had to make a quiet commitment. Ravenswood in Queensland was once the centre of a goldrush. When the rush died, the diggers flocked away, leaving an empty town to fall down. That was half a century ago. Just a few residents refused to conform and stayed. In this tiny town may be seen the tragic romance of human hope: it was built, lived in and abandoned all within the lifetime of its oldest resident, a lady who runs the Imperial Hotel. For eighty-one of her eighty-three years she has lived in Ravenswood.

A clutch of buildings still stands. The country around them is like a forgotten battlefield. Monumental lumps of machinery lie broken and abandoned, rusting into the landscape; a loose flap of iron squeals in the wind, listened to by a committee of crows. The clean air of human absence sweeps through the place, up towards the cemetery. Here gravestones, not so very old after all, crumble and collapse. The standing ones address a slope of slag pocked with neglected mineshafts, dead hopes, heat burning all colour from the grass, patches of red soil vivid among weeds and an empty beer bottle lying on its side. Here Di Barton, wife of Hugh, was buried in 1905 aged fifty-seven. 'Her kind deeds live on', the inscription says. With whom, one wonders.

Then the cemetery gate opens and an elderly lady, followed by her elderly son, walks in. She wears a straw hat, blouse and skirt, and carries a basket crammed with flowers unbelievably lush in this barren setting. She walks along the pathways, stopping now and again to distribute posies on various family graves. Her son fills the vases with fresh water from a plastic flagon. So many more dead than alive, one can't help thinking. The task of survival for those who refuse to move with the times can be immense and lonely. She places the last, brilliant stem of geranium in the pot on Di Barton's grave.

There are some things the comfortable majority will never know.

1 *A family at Coober Pedy, South Australia relaxes in its home which has been hollowed out of the very stuff in which the famous opals are found. The lure of wealth is but one of the reasons that people give for living in this intolerably hot, arid environment out in the Stuart Range; another, frequently stated, is the freedom of life so far from the urban masses.*

1

2   *Light plays across the lovely fragmented spectrum of colours in raw gem opals. Almost all the world's opal comes from Australia — not only from Coober Pedy but from areas such as Lightning Ridge, source of the highly-prized black opal.*

Migrants,
Willing and Less Willing

Twenty years ago, when I first let my beard grow, I was bailed up by a drunk in Brisbane who yelled into my face, 'What are you, a bloody Dago or something?' When I asked him what he meant he offered to bash my nose in for me. The most remarkable thing is that I don't recall being surprised by this behaviour. If it happened now, I would be absolutely astonished.

When asked what difference migrants have made to Australia, I am tempted to say, 'First they made us prejudiced, then they civilised us.' But this, of course, would be an overstatement. The point is that we were once an insulated Anglo-Celtic community. Having packed the remaining Aborigines out of sight on reserves, we could get on with our western style of life, reassured that the Indonesians were governed by nice safe Dutch people, Malaysians by the English, New Caledonians by the French. It was a European colonial club. We ourselves ruled New Guinea. Then, after the Second World War, all such cultural insulation fell apart. The neighbouring countries fought for their independence and got it. So now we were dealing directly with Papua New Guineans, Indonesians and Malaysians. To complicate the system further, a huge influx of Greek and Italian migrants and British migrants on assisted passages suddenly arrived looking for a place to live, a place to work and, even more challengingly, a place to belong. The community reacted, often with alarm.

This was a generation ago. Today, sons and daughters of these 'New Australians', as the euphemism went, are attending expensive private schools and wondering how they are going to adjust to the influx of Vietnamese. Indo-Chinese refugees now comprise the largest single migrant group at present entering Australia, but we accept refugees from forty countries, ranging from those escaping repression of the right in Chile or South Africa to those escaping repression of the left in Poland. Even so, the actual numbers coming are not so very high, but in the case of Asians, the public is especially aware of them because they are easy to recognise.

The latest census statistics list all persons of Asian origin as representing 8.4% of migrants born overseas. By comparison, Greeks

Darwin's exuberant Bougainvillea Festival reflects the cultural diversity of this city. Its population of 62 000 boasts forty-seven different racial and cultural backgrounds. The Chinese have always made up a major part of its population. Many can trace their roots in Australia back for over 100 years when their forefathers came to Darwin in the 1870s to help lay the telegraph line linking Australia with the rest of the world. Present-day immigrants from South-east Asia include refugees from Timor, Vietnam and Kampuchea.

represent 4.9%, Yugoslavians 5%, New Zealanders 5.9%, Italians 9.2% and British plus Irish 37.7%. The point so often overlooked is that most refugees, of whatever origin, hope to go back home eventually when conditions change there. The Vietnamese are no exception.

The irony has always been that intentions are so frequently thwarted by time. From an Aboriginal point of view, the entire white population is a migrant population. Neither the convicts, nor the redcoats of the New South Wales Corps, nor the administrators had the least intention of remaining beyond the compulsory time they were made to stay. Yet many of them never went back to Great Britain — either because they couldn't afford it or because they discovered a new life here which they were not prepared to leave.

The story was much the same for those who flocked to the country for the goldrushes of the 1850s and 1860s. Most, apart from the Chinese, stayed on, though they may never have intended doing so. This is still happening. Klaus Uhlenhut, for example, was twenty-two and a qualified dental technician working in Hanover when he saw an advertisement for tradesmen particularly sought as migrants

1   *The popular myth of the 'typical Australian' is sorely challenged by reality: this Melbourne crowd watching the Moomba Parade underscores the fact that today Australia is a cultural melting-pot. Names such as Koukoulis and Cheng are becoming as familiar as O'Connor and Jones.*

2   *Pretty as a doll and one of the crowd.*

3   *Anna Groeneveld listening to pupils reading at a school in the Melbourne suburb of Prahran. Learning English is often the first hurdle the new immigrant must face.*

1

2

3

to Australia. To his surprise, his own trade was listed. This planted the idea. Adventurous enough to feel he was already mouldering into a stagnant security, he sold his furniture, took the plunge and came. He was not an assisted migrant. He was not, he thought, a migrant at all. The plan was to travel through Asia en route and live in Australia for a couple of years at most.

He arrived in Darwin where he worked as a labourer. Afterwards, he made his way to Queensland and the Great Barrier Reef where he found a job as a gardener at the Dunk Island resort. Following his amateur fascination with natural history, he began systematically cataloguing and photographing the spiders he found on the island. Eventually, the management employed him to take guests for guided nature walks. He has been here two and a half years. He has no plans to remain permanently, but none to leave either. The only other job in Australia he admits he might be tempted by, is on a snake farm north of Cairns.

For many adventurous young people the story has been similar. And for some reason — whether because they fall in love and get married or because circumstances at home change — they have stayed. Others, who arrived with the expectation of settling permanently, have often found that Australia falls short of the promises. No easy road to wealth opens up. They miss their friends and relatives and the familiar life; some pack and go home. The population is a constant flux.

A generation ago, one could confidently sum up the Australian character in a few words (as many writers and politicians did) because the overwhelming majority came from the same national stock. Nowadays, the situation is far more complex. A brief glance at the roll of an average state school in any of the main cities well illustrates this point.

Kealba High School, in an outer Melbourne suburb, is typical enough to offer some insight into the present structure of society and what lies ahead for the nation at large. With a total enrolment of 950 students, over twenty different nationalities are represented. Sixty per cent of students come from migrant homes where English is not the main language spoken. In a survey of the students in 1982 they were counted according to ethnic background:

Anglo-Celtic: 195	Dutch: 5	Finnish: 1
Maltese: 86	Timorese: 5	French: 1
Yugoslavian: 86	Arabic: 3	Rumanian: 1
Greek: 75	Hungarian: 2	Russian: 1
Italian: 36	Filipino: 2	Thai: 1
Spanish: 16	Polish: 2	(Those with Australian
German: 14	Afrikaans: 1	parents: 403)
Turkish: 13	Albanian: 1	

Ninety-six of these students were born overseas. If we are ever to see the much talked-about multiculturalism, surely it will be here. Undoubtedly the possibility is present. Multi-nationalism we certainly already have in a school like this. But multiculturalism involves a two-way interaction. While all the pupils at Kealba High School have to learn English and Anglicised ways of life, the fact that they will never speak Finnish to the Finn or Greek to the Greeks, will never learn the manners of the Maltese or the decorum of the Arabs, ensures that multiculturalism will remain as elusive as ever. Perhaps it is more a pious intention than a practical expectation.

What we do expect is that these various nationalities will enrich that fluctuating concept, 'the Australian way of life'. In no area has

1 *For tangible evidence of the dividends of cultural diversity, nothing matches the numerous food markets in Australia. This smallgoods stall in sprawling Victoria Market, Melbourne, is redolent with garlic salamis, piquant sausages and a dazzling array of delicacies. The traditionally plain Australian diet has been revolutionised by delights as various as Peking duck, rich pink taramasalata, delicate Marscapone cheese and fruits and vegetables such as fresh dates and lychees.*

1

2

2   *A girl at Fremantle Markets, Western Australia, indulges in the national passion for icecreams and gelati. Only recently has the news leaked out to the rest of the world that Australia is a gourmet's paradise. Melbourne is justly touted as one of the food capitals of the world and maintains friendly competition with Sydney whose restaurants and food markets are equally famous.*

this expectation been more fulsomely justified than in food and wine. German settlers in South Australia have contributed enormously to the sophistication of wine-making; while restaurants of every nationality from Lebanese to Mexican, from French to Thai can be found in our cities. The markets are rich with the variety of vegetables and smallgoods immigrant people grow, make and buy. Little by little each exotic addition to the accepted range becomes part of the everyday experience. And the old, prim attitudes are sloughed off with relief.

Thirty years ago most Australian cities had Chinese restaurants, some with excellent food. On any one day I would see a few other European patrons eating with chopsticks. But what has changed is the *attitude* of the public. At the time, eating with chopsticks was thought to be a lark; next it was thought normal, now it is almost a statement. Self-conscious worldliness is part of the new national image. Who can tell what may lie beyond this? With any luck, a point where everybody welcomes the full variety and colour to be found in our community — and accepts this as one's own.

1, 2 *On 6th January each year the head of the Greek Orthodox Church in Melbourne (here Archbishop Panteleimon) officiates at the Blessing of the Fleet at Frankston, a bayside suburb of Melbourne. In full regalia and accompanied by a festive crowd carrying both the Greek and Australian flags, he performs the ceremony which is steeped in the rich traditions of the Mediterranean. Melbourne has the largest Greek population outside of Athens and Salonika.*

RELAXIN

Defining Ourselves Facing the Future

People the world over have this much in common; they need stories, music, rituals and a history to explain to themselves who they are and where they belong in the greater order. Lacking a religion deeply rooted in the soil, white Australians have tended to look to adventurers and artists to interpret and explain their identity. In the nineteenth century the two greatest clarifiers were a bushranger and a writer: Ned Kelly and Henry Lawson whose Australia, though still part of the modern reality, is only a part. Each generation must come to terms with its own character and actions.

The greatest of our living artists, the novelist Patrick White, presents a harsh view of his fellow countrymen on the whole. But that harshness is ennobled by an exploration of spiritual values through moral conflict. No artist achieved this for Australia before; it seemed as impossible as it might if we had no such values. But once there between two covers, it was immediately accepted — at least by the few.

In masterpieces on a grand scale (*Voss* and *Riders in the Chariot*) and on a smaller scale (*The Solid Mandala* and *A Fringe of Leaves*) he grapples with great issues, questioning the meaning of life in terms of explorers in our desert and the desert of our conformity, the conflict of white and Aboriginal culture, as well as weighing the world of the articulate against the insights of the mentally handicapped. He even creates a convincing allegory of the crucifixion in a suburban setting, acted out with passionate and chilling ferocity by ordinary Australian suburbanites driven by 'the authentic spasm' of racism and hatred against one who 'did not appear anything but fully informed'. Patrick White's achievement was recognised internationally when he was awarded the 1973 Nobel Prize for Literature.

Another artist of stature who has brilliantly interpreted the Australian experience is Lloyd Rees, now eighty-nine and the doyen of painters in this country. He was born in Brisbane during a period of tremendous floods, and so vivid were his memories of the wreckage that seventy-five years later, he was still drawing scenes

The secret of the human hormone, Relaxin, revealed in all its marvellous complexity. Dr H.D. Niall, Associate Director of the Howard Florey Institute, Melbourne, poses with a model of the hormone which was synthesised without ever having been isolated in pure form. Earlier work at the Institute on animal Relaxins laid the groundwork for this breakthrough which marks the first time that the structure of a molecule has been determined in this way. The significance goes far beyond the theoretical. Relaxin is vital in childbirth where it softens and lengthens the ligaments of the cervix and pelvis. It is hoped that this artificial hormone will help cut down injuries to infants during difficult deliveries.

from this time. Lloyd Rees went to Europe and perfected a classical technique which bears comparison with the great masters of Renaissance drawing. His interpretations of the Australian landscape and cities carry real authority. They also sing with the lyricism possible only to an artist who loves what he is painting. In his autobiography he offers a rhapsodic view of his birthplace, Brisbane, very much in the style of his paintings: 'From Mount Coot-tha the light galvanized roofs of the creamy-painted houses resembled large tents — myriads of them spread on both sides of the winding river, each house separate from its neighbour and most of them embowered in trees, the lovely jacaranda predominating. At dusk, with the jacarandas in bloom, the scene, a vision in silver and mauve-blue, was breathtaking in its beauty.'

Today, we take for granted not only that the country is beautiful, but that we have a character independent from any other people and that we have a history of our own. All this is a remarkably recent development. For the first fifty years from 1788 you could search in vain for a celebration of the beauty of the bush, though writers spent many a long, nostalgic page eulogising the English hedgerows and woods. The first historian to accord Australian history all the richness and excitement offered by the human experience is still living, still working on his monumental history, which he began to publish in 1962 and has now reached Volume 6 — Manning Clark. And if Professor Clark's tone rises at times to the grandiose, why not? He is speaking of a nation justly famous for its skites, after all. His magnificent work has put paid to the apologetic tone of so many of his predecessors.

The resurgence in Australian film-making is also having a powerful influence on national self-awareness. Australians have always had a touch of the 'Cultural Cringe' — denigrating anything local — so the financial success of many of our movies in England

1 *Kath Walker, Aboriginal poet, at her home. In the early 1960s she burst onto the Australian scene with her first book of poems 'We Are Going'. Her writing, filled with fearless passion, pummelled the wakening conscience of white Australians.*

2 *Manning Clark, the man who changed the emphasis of history in this country from a strictly British colonial viewpoint to a determinedly Australian one. He was the first historian to acknowledge the optimism Australians were beginning to feel for their land. He is still working on his 'History of Australia'. He originally planned to get it all into two volumes; he is currently working on volume six.*

3 *Prolific, sensitive and acutely attuned to the Australian landscape, Judith Wright is one of our outstanding poets.*

4 *Patrick White won the 1973 Nobel Prize for Literature. Works such as 'Voss', 'The Solid Mandala' and 'A Fringe of Leaves' ensure his place in the pantheon of modern literary masters.*

2

3

4

and the USA has brought about a positive euphoria at home. Film-makers are bursting with ideas and enthusiasm. The fresh approach of *The Cars that Ate Paris* and *Letters from Teralba Road* has won deserved recognition, just as the box-office romanticism of *Picnic at Hanging Rock* and *Breaker Morant* has led to international success.

The birth of a new nationalism affects all the arts. In music, composers are working more confidently than ever before. Richard Meale, with his intense orchestral works noted for their pungent and shimmering climaxes, is a remarkable presence. Again, he has won world acclaim, yet his music explores a strong sense of location — not just an interpretation of this land and its sounds, but weaving into its fabric sonorities from the Pacific region and Asia. Many of his colleagues have also dipped into Asian traditions to enrich their own.

Where composers tend to turn to Japanese and Javanese classical music for their influences, writers and painters incline more to India and China. In October 1983 a striking exhibition opened in Melbourne, Andrew Sibley's twenty-two paintings on the theme 'The Circus'. Indian elements in this very Australian show were clearly evident in the exuberant frieze of bodies. This major work presents a composite image for society as a whole, seen through the lens of personal relationships. These are insights no other artist has shown in quite the same way: poignant and penetrating, terrible and tender. Sibley presents us with paintings that are not just about people in tinsel costumes, but about a passionate struggle against despair, about the lethal rivalry of those who consume and those who are consumed. It is a view of ourselves many might find uncomfortable.

Science, by comparison, is regarded as much more comforting, which is paradoxical considering the massive destructive developments during this century. The common feeling is that

1 Working from designs specially created for them, artist-craftsmen and women at the Victorian Tapestry Workshop apply their skills to interpreting this design by Richard Larter. The work was commissioned by the Australian National Gallery where it now hangs. Of the four major tapestry centres in the world today, the Victorian Tapestry Workshop is considered by many to represent 'the state of the art', yet its achievements are hardly known to the average Australian.

2 Close-up of 'Pretty As' by Richard Larter and the Victorian Tapestry Workshop.

3 Visitors to the Heide Gallery, Bulleen, Victoria. Australia's landscapes and uncompromising light have proved a challenge to artists. They have had to put aside sensibilities conditioned by Europe and strike out on their own. Artists such as Lloyd Rees, Sir Russell Drysdale and Fred Williams have impelled Australian art onto a new path.

4 Andrew Sibley with one of the twenty-two paintings on the theme 'The Circus'.

2

3

4

whatever problems science creates, science can also solve. People will admit that, on one hand, the perils of nuclear technology may have outstripped the political sophistication to manage them wisely; but on the other, they feel there is genuine cause for excitement at our research programmes.

The Commonwealth Scientific and Industrial Research Organization (CSIRO) has been central to the government's policy of financing research. Among the most recent successes has been the development of effective biological insecticides that are non-toxic to other wildlife, a new system of spinning worsted weaving yarns so that they can compete better with synthetics, the Sirofloc water purification system (which already supplies five per cent of Perth's needs), and development of an instrument to detect wear and faults in steel-reinforced conveyor belts used in the mining industry.

Another area of tremendous advancement has been in the field of radio astronomy; the CSIRO together with the University of Tasmania, using the radio telescope at Parkes, NSW, discovered pulsars in the earth's nearest galaxy.

1   *The Human Veins Dance Theatre, based in Canberra, performing 'Oresteia' at the Melbourne Concert Hall.*

2   *Interior of the Concert Hall, Sydney Opera House.*

3   *In rehearsal, students of the Victorian College of the Arts School of Dance. The classical, international influence is readily apparent in Australian ballet but change is afoot. The work of people such as Graeme Murphy marks a fresh, innovative — and very Australian — approach.*

1

2

3

At universities and research institutes throughout the country new work is going on. Perhaps one of the most important successes of late has been a revolutionary silicon chip design process that permits chips to be made to the exact specification of the purchaser and yet at a price that is a fraction of that by other mass-production methods. The significance for the manufacturing industry is immense.

A substantial part of the CSIRO budget is spent on agricultural projects: soil engineering for increased fertility, fresh approaches to insect and disease control, improved plant strains and animal breeds. But this is not to say that its interests are merely local. Research is taking place on subjects as diverse as aeronautics (Australian technology assisted in the successful Columbia space shuttle in America), entomology, paper-making and from radar to rain making, to possible uses for shark oil. A recent project to develop a ceramic resistant to rapid temperature changes has given Australia a stake in the development of new motor car components, for some prototypes have ceramic parts in place of the traditional metal ones. These new engines promise improved fuel economy.

The CSIRO is not the only source of scientific and technological innovation in the country. In university laboratories around the country discoveries are being made, ideas developed. Not all are reported in the press although breakthroughs such as the 'bionic ear' arouse public interest. This technique, developed at the University of Melbourne, promises to bring, for the first time, hearing to the profoundly deaf. The government recently granted $2 million to this project.

Microsurgery was developed in Australia, the work of Dr Earl Ronald Owen and Dr David Vickers. Not only did they develop the technique but also the tools with which to work. Dr Owen replaced the amputated finger of a small child in 1968 and since then such procedures have become all but commonplace the world over.

The recent synthesis of the hormone, Relaxin, marked another major breakthrough. It is the first time that a hormone has been artificially synthesised without the laborious process of first physically breaking apart the natural substance. This work, at the Howard Florey Institute in Melbourne, has a far-reaching application, for Relaxin is a vital hormone that controls the ligaments of the pelvis during childbirth. It is expected to bring down the incidence of cerebral palsy which so often results from difficult births.

More dramatic has been the development in Australia of *in vitro* fertilisation. Australia's first 'in vitro' baby, Candice Reed, was born in Melbourne in June 1980 and her arrival triggered wide-spread controversy.

The words *in vitro* simply mean 'in glass'; the ova from the mother-to-be are removed and fertilised by sperm from the man. These fertilised eggs (usually two to four of them) are then allowed to develop briefly in a glass container and, when the doctors are satisfied that fertilisation has taken place, the eggs are implanted in the mother's womb. After this, the pregnancy progresses normally.

So far there have been well over a hundred IVF births in Melbourne and obstetricians and gynaecologists the world over have come to Australia to study these techniques.

Public response has been fiercely divided. Many have hailed it as a marvel. Others condemn it because of religious objections and

1   *Gillian Armstrong, right, against the poster for her film 'Starstruck'. This followed on her acclaimed 'My Brilliant Career' which confirmed her status as a successful director. She is an example of the talent nurtured by the Australian Film and Television School.*

2   *Bullamakanka, one of the top country music groups, playing at the Night Hawks Club, Cairns.*

3   *On the set of 'Phar Lap' which became an instant box-office success.*

1

2

3

moral repugnance at the interference with a natural process. Searching questions arise from the fact that sperm from more than one man can be used in the fertilisation. There is also the accusation of sexism based on the argument that if the sperm can come from other sources than the father, need the ova come from the mother? The prospect of genetic engineering looms in the future, arousing fears that these techniques have already outstripped our wisdom in managing them.

The issue has been taken seriously enough, at least in Victoria, for the state government to set up a committee of enquiry. Meanwhile, research continues, presenting yet more challenges. One of the most contentious is the freezing of the embryo (with the patient's consent) which may then be thawed and implanted at a later date. The most powerful media image in favour of 'in vitro' fertilisation is not a moral argument at all, but interviews with joyful parents who had lost hope of having children of their own.

Australian research, with little scope for application at home, already brings benefits to millions of people overseas. The Walter and Eliza Hall Institute in Melbourne achieved international acclaim for immunological research when it was directed by Sir Macfarlane Burnet, who was awarded a Nobel Prize for his work; and it is still at the forefront. Under the present director, Professor Sir Gustav Nossal, encouraging progress has been made in the elusive search for a malaria vaccine. This remarkable effort, conducted in conjunction with the Institute of Medical Research at Madang in New Guinea, promises to bring relief to more than 150 million people throughout the world. The implications of this breakthrough have been hailed by the World Health Organisation.

Research, by its nature, looks to the future. There are many programmes already well-advanced that we seldom hear about, which may be looked on as milestones by generations to come. But Australian business has a poor record for putting money into the application of Australian discoveries. Many research projects are simply registered and left unused. Others, after being turned down by local investors, are snapped up by foreign companies. And, of course, the chief economic benefit of inventions comes at the fabrication stage. The present Minister for Science and Technology,

1 Deep in the Australian outback, the Nomad Film Company crew shoots a scene for 'The Pintubi'. Documentaries by this company have been distributed worldwide and have been greatly acclaimed.

2 David Gulpilil was plucked from anonymity in his native Arnhem Land to star in the famous Australian film, 'Walkabout'.

3 Jack Thompson first caught the public eye in the brilliant film 'Sunday Too Far Away'. Since that 1975 success, he has featured in such Australian classics as 'The Man From Snowy River' and 'Breaker Morant'.

4 Bryan Brown, here amid blood and dust on the set of 'Eureka Stockade', is one of the most sought-after leading men.

5 On the set of 'Prisoner', one of the highest-rating continuing television dramas in Australia. Focusing on social issues, particularly as they affect women, the predominantly female cast continues to hold its audiences. As the industry as a whole has matured, its programmes have won increasing favour overseas while remaining immensely popular at home.

Barry Jones, constantly campaigns for more public money to be spent on research and for better communication with the business community in the hope that private investment in Australian ideas will increase. Otherwise, we are doomed to fall behind in the high-technology market-place and become little more than a source of raw materials for rival nations so they can forge yet further ahead of us. His point is underscored by the fact that though two per cent of world research is done in this country, a dismal 0.1 per cent of high technology applications are Australian. That we can do better is demonstrated by the success of the ventures which are financed. The Sydney company Systems Technology, for example, signed a multi-million dollar contract in 1983 to export talking computers to Japan — of all places. And D. D. Webster Electronics has received orders from the USA for its Spectrum II mini-computer to aid design development in the plastics industry; customers include such firms as IBM and RCA.

Sir Gustav Nossal has added his voice to this challenge to industry to capitalise on discoveries being made in Australia. He points out that the future of medical research lies in the field of biotechnology and that the products should be developed and manufactured in this country. Modern cell biology could well lead researchers to knowledge of how to combat cancer; already great advances have been made in investigating cancer genes and intercellular interaction. The point is, when this scientific investigation comes up with some practical answers, who is going to develop them as products, test, manufacture and market them worldwide? He urges scientists to take development work more seriously and industry to allot a greater proportion of profits to fund research. In Sir Gustav's words, 'Because of the separate development of science and technology in Australia, we have inherited a scientific structure where experimental development and applied research are not being

1 *1984 marked the birth of Australia's Medicare system which will provide free medical care for every citizen, from this infant in intensive care to the old and disabled, irrespective of income. Medicare was brought into being by the Labor Government which is committed to changing and improving welfare services.*

2 *Members of the now famous Melbourne 'in vitro' fertilisation team (Queen Victoria Medical Centre, Epworth Hospital, Monash University), performing a laparoscopy on a prospective mother. Using fine optical equipment to guide them, they remove ripe ova which are then fertilised with sperm in a glass container. Within three days cell division begins, the fertilised ovum is implanted back into the mother and the pregnancy proceeds normally.*

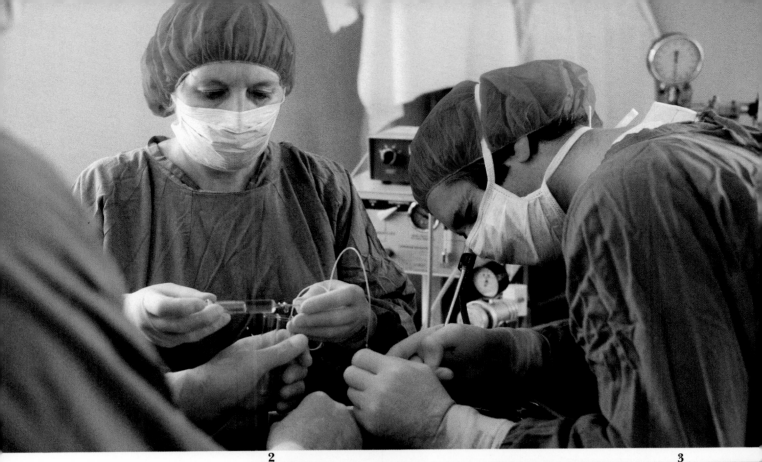

2

3

3   Sperm from husbands and donors, carefully labelled and frozen in liquid nitrogen for later use. The moral and ethical issues of IVF are still being hotly debated, but the research continues and endless possibilities emerge. Recent work using frozen embryos is particularly controversial. While it can allow women without functioning ovaries to be implanted with donated fertilised ova, the procedure could also be applied to genetic tampering or to creating a super-race.

4   Carl Wood (left) and Alan Trounson (right) the two men who headed the development of IVF in Melbourne. When Candice Reed, the first Australian 'test-tube' baby, made her appearance in June 1980, she gave hope to thousands of people who had despaired of ever having children of their own.

4

pursued with sufficient vigour, and where industry has left too big a proportion of the financial burden with government.'

Credit must go to the government for the scientific output we have had and for much of the artistic output as well. Through the Australia Council, writers, composers, painters and sculptors are now able to apply for generous support while they work, just as scientists are governmentally supported at the CSIRO and by the education budget through the universities' grants. So the question is not just whether the business community will pick up its share of the bill but whether present and future governments will expand these programmes, or yield to the ever-present sniping of those citizens whose imaginations cannot stretch beyond the crudest commercialism — that you ought to be able to see what you buy, that any dollar spent on ideas is a dollar thrown away.

1   *The immense dish of the deep-space communication centre at Tidbinbilla, near Canberra, ACT, against a stormy night sky.*

2   *The European settlement of Australia can be attributed, at least in part, to astronomy. James Cook's original mandate on his 1768-71 voyage included the task of tracking the transit of Venus, a phenomenon visible only in the southern hemisphere. Since then Australia's southern vantage-point, climatic conditions and up-*

1

2

3

to-date technology have made her a world leader in the field. This stellar intensity interferometer is at Narrabri, New South Wales.

3   Tackling the problem of disposing of nuclear waste, Professor Ted Ringwood devised Synroc — short for synthetic rock. Stabilising radioactive waste in Synroc and then burying it safely deep underground could provide a solution to one of the most worrying issues of the nuclear age. This important discovery has been patented and is being tested.

1

2

3

1 *A preview of things to come? Hans Tholstrup in the tiny solar car, 'Quiet Achiever', on its astonishing 4000-kilometre journey across the continent. Despite Australia's plentiful supply of solar energy, it is unlikely that this will be the car of the future. In order to power a normal-sized vehicle, an unwieldy number of solar cells would be necessary. As it is, the 150-kilogram vehicle averaged a valiant 24 kilometres per hour.*

2 *Hans Tholstrup who, with Larry Perkins made the 20-day crossing of the continent, with well-wishers on his arrival in Sydney.*

3 *Tagging koalas is not for the faint-hearted. A researcher sets about capturing a koala which will be examined, fitted with a radio collar and then released back into the bush. As more and more gum trees are felled, the koala's future becomes less secure, for its survival depends on a diet of eucalypt leaves.*

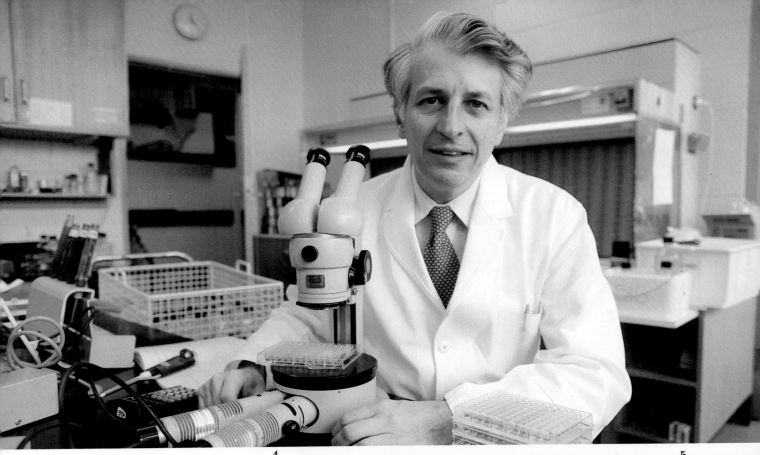

4   *Sir Gustav Nossal, Director of the Walter and Eliza Hall Institute, is outspoken on the future of medical research. He points out that while biotechnology is the area of main development in the future, Australia's research often leads nowhere simply because too few business people are prepared to test, manufacture and market the products of this work. To date, much of the burden of research and development has rested with the Government.*

5   *Aboard one of the planes of the famous 'flying doctor' service that brings medical care to Australia's widely scattered outback population. Since 1980 the service has handled an astonishing 100 000 calls for medical help and an estimated 8000 people have been air-lifted to hospital.*

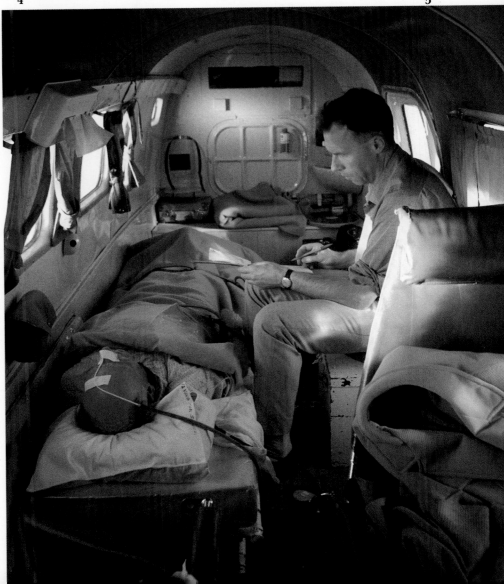

Feasts and Festivals

Winton is a small town in central Queensland. The country there is extremely flat, extremely hot and dusty, and it is remote. Yet it has its claim to celebrity: Dagworth Station, where the poet Banjo Paterson wrote his words for the nation's unofficial and most-loved anthem, *Waltzing Matilda*. Accordingly, Winton now holds a Banjo Paterson Festival. One young bushman explained the advantages to me: 'There's great potential for developing tourism in the outback. I mean, Winton's real scrub. There's nothing there!'

Australia's great festivals are the agricultural shows, horse races, the Victorian Football League's Grand Final, the Sydney-Hobart yacht race and Anzac Day. They have this much in common: they take place outdoors and they celebrate either the abundance of food, or physical prowess in one form or another. Not one is religious or political. Christmas is a family feast. Easter, Australia Day and Labor Day are all observed as days off work but very little more.

The element of religion adds solemnity to Anzac Day but it does not take over from the principal focus — honouring the men and women who died at war, and the memories of those who survived. Perhaps the reason is that religion is seen as divisive; the country has a history of barely suppressed and often bitter rivalry between Roman Catholics and Protestants. All round Australia just before dawn, at the same time as the Anzac troops made their landing at Gallipoli on 25 April 1915, these essentially secular services begin.

In Brisbane, crowds gather in Anzac Park among the bottle trees, the handsome street lamps still glow. In the solemn hush they look up towards the Shrine of Remembrance where dignitaries have gathered at the top of the twin curving stairways. The Shrine itself is a circle of doric columns open to the morning; a flame burns there, fluttering, pale blue as the coming dawn itself. Those who will later march through the city, some in their best suits, others in open-necked shirts adorned with clinking medals, bow their heads. The sky lightens, someone in the crowd coughs quietly. The service is simple and moving. When the bugler sounds the *Last Post* a moment of feeling touches the crowd, like a benediction.

Each Chinese New Year, a rippling dragon decked in crimson and gold cavorts down Little Bourke Street in Melbourne's Chinatown. The street throngs with revellers — not only people of Chinese descent, but a host of others along for the fun.

Later in the day, old comrades-in-arms hold their reunions, reminisce about battles in their increasingly distant youth and, in some cases, get drunk. This, above all days, is the occasion for celebrating the old Australia and for an open affirmation of being Australian. That in itself, for an undemonstrative people, is an emotional event.

Religious days, apart from Christmas, have no such unifying aspect. On the contrary, the exciting diversity of our people is apparent in the plethora of minority religious festivals. The Greek Easter and Russian Easter fall on a different date than the Catholic and Protestant Easter, and the richness of their rituals is even more sumptuous. Jewish and Muslim people, Chinese, Turks, Armenians and Latvians — to name but a few — all have their own religious observances. The only pity is that they are not encouraged to bring their festivities out into the street as they would in their homelands, enriching the life of the whole nation.

Some quite secular festivals have an ethnic flavour too. The Barossa Valley Vintage Festival in South Australia began as the traditional European thanksgiving for the harvest. The winegrowers first gathered together in 1947 to celebrate among themselves. Now, every second year, it is a major commercial enterprise. The German families are very strong in the district, with Henschke, Blass, Thumm, Liebich and Seppelt among the most famous. Small town streets are decorated with bunting for the folk dancing, for the strassenfest, kellerfest and general gemutlichkeit.

If the Barossa Festival celebrates production, the Canberra Wine and Food Frolic blatantly celebrates consumption. Held in the heat of January, it is a shameless blow-out. The citizens flock to Commonwealth Gardens, pay for a ticket, and circulate round the stalls sampling everything they can stuff in, from exotic cooking to vintage wines — the much-publicised Australian hedonism rampant.

The fertility of the soil is the central theme of agricultural shows across the land. These shows, held in small towns and large alike, are perhaps the greatest and most sustained of Australian festivals. Huge numbers of people from the country as well as the city flock to see the combination of practical exhibits of farm machinery with funfair amusements. Loud speakers echo, kids tear about in crazy hats, teenagers squeal as they are whirled through heart-stopping gyrations in the amusements alley, and out in the arena, sheep-dog trials and camp-drafting test worker-skills of men and women on the land. The pavilions, too, celebrate productivity including many of the skills of the farmer's wife such as baking, knitting and jam making.

The great centrepiece of the Show in each capital city is the Grand Parade. Cattle and horses file onto the ground from opposite ends. Led by their respective grand champions, they form concentric circles, rotating in contrary directions. By the time the whole huge, shifting, dynamic tableau is assembled the effect is magnificent: with the winners decked in brilliant ribbons and champion trotters high-stepping it round the outer track. But the curious truth is that in so huge a gathering of prize beasts, sheep, pigs, goats and all, there is no animal native to Australia.

Where the agricultural shows draw country people to the city, the best of the arts festivals attract city people from other states. The Perth Festival and Adelaide Festival of Arts both cater for visitors

1   *Thousands of Melburnians gather for the annual Carols by Candlelight at the Sidney Myer Music Bowl. This glorious venue with its concrete roof like the sheltering wings of a dove, was bequeathed to the citizens by the founder of the Myer Emporium — a company which changed the face of retail trading in Australia.*

2   *Every State and Territory has its festivals. They range from Adelaide's prestigious Festival of the Arts which attracts people countrywide to its glorious performances of music, drama, poetry readings, ballet and opera to Melbourne's Moomba with its emphasis on entertainment and sheer high spirits.*

3   *A church service on the Greek Easter is imbued with rich ritual and symbolism. Such religious occasions seem to belong to the many minority groups rather than to the mainstream whose attendance at universal celebrations with a religious content has diminished.*

1

2

3

1 *Amid pomp and flowers, Canberra honours Anzac Day.*

2 *Nurses who served in World War 2 parade in Adelaide.*

3 *The music-hall style of entertainment from World War 2 evokes tears and memories at the Returned Servicemen's League hall on Anzac Day in Cairns.*

4 *One of the thousands of Australians who saw active service.*

5 *The keynote of Anzac Day: 'We will remember them lest we forget.' At Cairns earlier that morning the march to the cenotaph took place, the dawn silence broken only by the shuffling of feet and clinking of medals.*

3

4

5

intending to saturate themselves in music, drama, exhibitions, poetry readings, ballet and opera. The programmes are built round a core of international performers (different each time) of the very highest calibre, from the Royal Shakespeare Company to the Israel Philharmonic Orchestra to the Bunraku Puppet Theatre of Japan.

The Adelaide Festival began in 1960 and its basis was strictly commercial. The Lord Mayor called a meeting of 'public-spirited' businessmen to ask each of them for a £15 000 guarantee before launching a public appeal. 'As the purpose of the festival,' he pointed out, 'is to add to the prestige of Adelaide and bring more visitors to the city, with increased business, most firms will be able to charge any costs to expenses in the usual way.' They brought out the director of the Edinburgh Festival to advise them, and success was immediate. There is no question that it has added to Adelaide's prestige and brought a lot of people and a lot of money to the city.

Among the most regular performers at these arts festivals are our two stage extravaganzas, the Australian Ballet Company and the Australian Opera. Even playing away from their respective home theatres in Melbourne and Sydney, they bring something of a gala feeling with them. Lavishly costumed and glitteringly lit, they represent very much the standard repertoire expected of similar companies in London or New York. Great stars such as Rudolf Nureyev and Luciano Pavarotti lend further glamour. And the opera company's Dame Joan Sutherland is the resident prima donna.

At the opposite end of the spectrum are the anti-cultural celebrations of ockerdom. Most ocker of all is Darwin's Beer Can Regatta. This wild, boozy event is held every June. The competing 'boats' are backyard contraptions made entirely of empty beer cans. Darwin offers an unsurpassed supply of raw materials. Everything from rafts to fancy structures boasting poop decks and echoes of the Spanish Main, they paddle out to sea and back, manned by raucous crews of drinkers emptying yet more cans to assure the future of the event.

A half degree more refined is the Alice Springs 'Henley-on-Todd Regatta'. This zany parody of aquatic sports is held in a dry river bed. The main event, the eights, could scarcely be further from the graceful rowing race its name suggests. Eight team members run through heavy sand, the bottomless 'boat' frame joggling and wobbling round them. The joke about lack of water suggests a touch of stoicism — Alice Springs being right out in the Central Australian desert. And the celebrations have a hysterical edge: the men wearing naval fancy dress, sporting life-jackets and carrying surfboards, admire the bathing beauties while barracking for mates in the keel-hauling and lifesaving events. The one disaster the organisers insure against is the remote possibility of rain!

In this, like every other competition, gambling plays an important part. Australians are a betting people. Not to honour a bet is considered the lowest of low behaviour. From dog races to federal elections, you can always find somebody willing to offer odds and take a bet on the results. As a matter of pride, every small town runs its picnic races at least once a year. Larger places have weekly race meetings. One race, however, eclipses all the rest. It is an event of national importance — the Melbourne Cup.

Melbourne itself takes the day off as a holiday. And right throughout the country, the parliaments, courts, universities,

1 *There are few Australian sporting events as infectiously exuberant as the Victorian Football League Grand Final. Here the umpire waves his white flags in an arcane semaphore understood by the hundreds of thousands of Australian devotees of this game. More aerial and balletic than soccer or rugby, Australian Rules has a fascination all of its own.*

2 *A Hawthorn supporter waves his team's colours.*

3 *Carlton (the Blues) v Collingwood (the Magpies) during the winter 'footy' season. Twelve teams hotly compete for the premiership.*

1

2

3

businesses, factories and shops come to a standstill at 2.40 p.m. for the race. Cup Day originated when Melbourne was the biggest and richest city in the land. In 1880, 100 000 people attended at a time when the city's population was 282 000. Gold was the basis of Victoria's boom years and gambling became near-as-damn-it a commitment to principle. The 1983 punters bet a mighty $60 million on the day.

Big sporting events of this kind celebrate the openness of Australian society, but they also reflect the power structure. The distinction between 'The Outer' and 'The Members' stands are kept up right round the nation. One suspects that the distinction matters more to those within than to those without.

The Melbourne Cup, with its kaleidoscope of extravagant fashions and the larrikin vitality of a betting crowd, is only surpassed by that other major event on the sporting calendar, the Victorian Football League Grand Final. The peculiar intensity of this game is due to its uniquely Melbourne character. Everyone shares intimate knowledge of the rules and who the players are. It is the one sport they know is exclusively theirs and they are convinced it is unparalleled among the world's ball games as a spectacle. (They are right!)

Faster and more open than any other code of football, there is no off-side and no scrum to bog the game down. It is aerial and free-flowing; a peculiar blend of discipline and anarchy, of brutal physical clashes and balletic elegance. The players do not look like soccer or rugby players — they are more sleek, lean and long-legged, wearing their sleeveless uniforms like a second skin. They are supremely narcissistic. Unlike other footballers they seem at least as much concerned with masculine beauty as with the actual points they score.

Unlike other sports, Victorian football does not turn to national and international competition. It is inward-looking, the whole twenty-six weeks of top-level competition are played mostly within the boundaries of Melbourne. The Final brings the people of the city together generating civic pride and identity in a way no sport or social ritual does for any other of our cities. Throughout the year it is the one topic of conversation that allows people to communicate

1, 2 Delighted with their trophy, winners at the 97th Race Meeting at Normanton in Queensland's Gulf Country. Out here the land is flat with more rivers than roads and the population is widely scattered. Normanton itself has fewer than a thousand citizens, but its race meetings bring everyone in the district together. And after the horses have pounded over the hot, dusty course, people from far and wide get together to chat, renew friendships, drink and exchange news.

3 Mysterious Hanging Rock creates a powerful backdrop to the famous picnic races that take place here in January each year. In the crowd, locals from the Macedon area rub shoulders with day-trippers from Melbourne who come out to picnic, punt on the horses and enjoy themselves.

2
3

despite social differences, providing ready-made introductions for strangers ('He's a Fitzroy supporter, but he's not a bad bloke all the same.') The 115 000 spectators at a Final and the players themselves are exhilarated and transformed by their part in the match.

Sydney sporting events, on the whole, are more directed towards participation than watching. This is especially true in surf contests, where the crowd loses its power of making a noise. At a VFL Grand Final the concerted sigh and the concerted roar of the people are thrilling in themselves. But on a beach where the surf perpetually thunders in, the spectators tend to be more introspective, their applause insignificant.

The main spectacle, however, is quite simply matchless. Each Boxing Day the nation's greatest sailing race sets out on its 1200-kilometre course from Sydney to Hobart. And the population of Sydney takes to the water in every conceivable kind of craft that will float. The gigantic harbour is crammed with sails, ferries, motorboats, rowing boats and even surf skis. The year I took my children to South Head to watch the vast flotilla of smallfry milling across the harbour and out to sea, one daughter looked up — illuminated with discovery — and said, 'This is where everything happened.' Yes, with sailing ships, on that occasion heading the other way, advancing through the Heads, and Governor Arthur Phillip enthusing in his dispatches that this was the finest harbour in the world.

As the big yachts race south, the well-wishers turn about and tack for home. They are the thousands who create the sense of occasion. Without them it would simply be the beginning of a race. The sight is all the more breathtaking for knowing that, beautiful as the boats look, they are beyond the safety limit, bobbing on the open sea. The last fanatics, reluctant to answer the call of land, hold the spectators on the clifftops spellbound long after the big yachts have gone.

1 *Wherever you are in Australia, horse racing is a passion. And no race evokes greater interest and excitement than the Melbourne Cup. The city takes a public holiday and at 2.40 pm on the day, the nation comes to a halt for the race. Glued to transistor radios and television screens, Australians throughout the country join Melburnians as the field of thoroughbreds competes for the purse. In brilliant silks, the jockeys return to the scales with their mounts at Flemington after the race.*

2 *Cup Day is traditionally an occasion to flaunt your idiosyncracies.*

3 *Patterned on the classic races of England, the Melbourne Cup has adopted the pre-race champagne picnic, too. In the Members' carpark, crystal, silver and tablecloths emerge from the boots of Rolls Royces and lavish hampers are unpacked.*

2

3

5

4 *Beaming jockey and owners of the winner of the 1983 Melbourne Cup hold their trophies.*

5 *Women in all their finery are as much a part of the Melbourne Cup scene today as they must have been in 1861 when the first race was run.*

4

Perhaps this, of all Australian festivals, brings the people most closely in touch with their boundaries, recalling the long perspective of history. Children and adults alike gaze out to sea, dumbfounded at the vastness and blueness of the South Pacific Ocean — suddenly aware they are standing on the edge of a great land.

1 *Enjoying the pleasures of the Sydney Easter Show, one of the largest of the many agricultural shows countrywide that celebrate the productivity of the land.*

2 *August in Alice Springs out in the Central Desert and a team of competitors in the Henley-on-Todd Regatta churn up the riverbed in their 'boat'. The organisers of this zany event take out insurance against rain filling the riverbed.*

SOUTHERN XX

3

3   Kid and a koala at
Dreamworld, a sprawling
amusement park 23 kilometres
north of Surfers' Paradise.

4   The Superloop — one of the
many rides at the Royal
Melbourne Show.

5   Floats go by to the delight of
the crowd at the Moomba Parade,
Melbourne.

4

5

1

2

3

4

Previous page 1 *A boardsurfer swept up by the exhilaration of 'the tube'. Australia's long coastline offers some of the finest surf beaches in the world and generations of Australians have honed their skills here before taking on — and beating — competition from all over the world.*

2 *Carrying their lifesaving reels, competing teams of surf lifesavers parade at a Surf Carnival. Surf-rescue originated in this country and has, unlike in North America, remained a voluntary association. The magnificently trained young men and women patrol popular swimming beaches and watch for trouble. The list of awards for bravery makes fascinating reading: gory stories of beating off shark attacks and bold bids to save swimmers swept far out to sea.*

3 *Female surf lifesavers such as these at Venus Bay, Victoria, are still a relatively novel sight for, until recently, it was a male preserve.*

4 *From an early age Australian youngsters take to the sea. Armed with gaily coloured boards, they are a familiar sight on the coast.*

This page: *Even on an overcast day, the start of the Sydney-to-Hobart yacht race is breathtaking. With Sydney as a backdrop, the harbour throngs with the graceful competitors and thousands of other craft there for the occasion. Long after the yachts themselves are out to sea on their perilous 1200-kilometre course south, the wellwishers linger on celebrating this spectacular event.*

181

Photographic Credits

	Ian McKenzie 2
	Gunther Deichmann, Talentbank 3
	Michael Coyne, Talentbank 4
94	David Moore
96/97	Carolyn Johns, Talentbank 1
	Michael Coyne, Talentbank 2
	Rennie Ellis, Scoopix 3
98/99	Rennie Ellis, Scoopix 1 2 3
100/101	David Moore
102/103	Rennie Ellis, Scoopix 1
	Ron Ryan, The Photo Agency, Melb. 2
	David Moore, Scoopix 3 5
	Robin Smith 4
104/105	Philip Quirk, Talentbank 1
	Ron Ryan, The Photo Agency, Melb. 2 4
	David Parker, Talentbank 3
106/107	Gunther Deichmann, Talentbank 1
	Ron Ryan, The Photo Agency, Melb. 2 3
	Rennie Ellis, Scoopix 4
108/109	Michael Coyne, Talentbank
110/111	Ron Ryan, The Photo Agency, Melb. 1 3
	Philip Quirk, Talentbank 2
	Michael Coyne, Talentbank 4
112/113	Michael Coyne, Talentbank 1
	Gunther Deichmann, 2 3 4
114/115	Robin Smith 1
	Bill Bachman, Scoopix 2
	Michael Coyne, Talentbank 3
	Peter Solness 4
116/117	Ron Ryan, The Photo Agency, Melb. 1 3
	Robin Smith 2
118/119	Rennie Ellis, Scoopix 1 2
	Ron Ryan, The Photo Agency, Melb. 3
120/121	Ron Ryan, The Photo Agency, Melb. 1 3
	Rennie Ellis, Scoopix 2 4
122/123	Ron Ryan, The Photo Agency, Melb. 1
	Gunther Deichmann 2 3 4
124/125	Ron Ryan, The Photo Agency, Melb. 1 2 3 4
126/127	Bill Bachman 1 3
	Robin Smith 2
128	Peter Solness
130/131	Roger Garwood 1 4
	Rennie Ellis, Scoopix 2 3
132/133	Rennie Ellis, Scoopix 1
	Philip Little, Scoopix 2
134/135	Keith Midson, The Photo Agency, Melb. 1
	Oliver Strewe, Talentbank 2
136/137	Milton Wordley, Talentbank 1 2
138	Gunther Deichmann
140/141	Ron Ryan, The Photo Agency, Melb. 1
	Richard Durham, The Photo Agency, Melb. 2
	Rennie Ellis, Scoopix 3
142/143	Ron Ryan, The Photo Agency, Melb. 1
	Peter Solness 2
144/145	Richard Durham, The Photo Agency, Melb. 1 2
146	Michael Coyne, Talentbank
148/149	Michael Coyne, Talentbank 1
	Tom Hollyman, Photo Researchers Inc. 2
	Australian Information Service, Canberra 3
	Austral International, Sydney 4
150/151	Rennie Ellis, Scoopix 1 2 3
	Dieter Muller 4
152/153	Australian Information Service, Canberra 1
	Don McMurdo 2
	Russel Naughton 3
154/155	Tom Hollyman, Talentbank 1
	Rennie Ellis, Scoopix 2
	David Parker, Talentbank 3
156/157	John Ogden, Nomad Films
	International 1
	David Moore 2
	Carolyn Johns, Talentbank 3
	David Parker, Talentbank 4
	Grundy Television Pty Ltd 5
158/159	Carolyn Johns, Talentbank 1
	David Parker, Talentbank 2 3 4
160/161	Ron Ryan, The Photo Agency, Melb. 1
	David Moore 2
	Australian Information Service, Canberra 3
162/163	Roger Garwood, Talentbank 1
	Andy Park, Talentbank 2
	Michael Coyne, Talentbank 3 4
	David Moore 5
164	Ron Ryan, The Photo Agency, Melb.
166/167	Richard Durham, The Photo Agency, Melb. 1
	Ron Ryan, The Photo Agency, Melb. 2
	Rennie Ellis, Scoopix 3
168/169	Ron Ryan, The Photo Agency, Melb. 1
	Milton Wordley, Talentbank 2
	Rennie Ellis, Scoopix 3 4 5
170/171	David G. Segal, Talentbank 1 2
	Ron Ryan, The Photo Agency, Melb. 3
172/173	Ron Ryan, The Photo Agency, Melb. 1 2 3
174/175	Ron Ryan, The Photo Agency, Melb. 1 2
	Rennie Ellis, Scoopix 3
	Michael Coyne, Talentbank 4 5
176/177	Peter Solness 1
	Scoopix 2
	Richard Durham, The Photo Agency, Melb. 3
	Ron Ryan, The Photo Agency, Melb. 4 5
178/179	Ian Crawford, Scoopix 1
	Ron Ryan, The Photo Agency, Melb. 2 3
	Oliver Strewe, Talentbank 4
180/181	Ron Ryan, The Photo Agency, Melb.